SpringerBriefs in Psychology

Best Practices in Cognitive-Behavioral Psychotherapy

Series Editors
Daniel David
Raymond A. DiGiuseppe
Kristene A. Doyle

More information about this series at http://www.springer.com/series/10143

Epidemiological studies show that the prevalence of mental disorders is extremely high across the globe (World Health Organization, 2011). Moreover, and what is perhaps more concerning is the fact that, despite numerous existing evidence-based treatments for various mental disorders, more than half of those in need of specialized mental health services don't access it and/or do not have access to these treatments (Alonso et al., 2004c; Kohn, Saxena, Levav, & Saraceno, 2004; Wang et al., 2005). Thus, developing and disseminating accessible evidence-based protocols for various clinical conditions are key goals in mental health. This effort would nicely complement the efforts of the American Psychological Association (see Division 12's List of evidence-based treatments), National Institute for Health and Clinical Excellence (see NICE's Guidelines) and Cochrane Reviews (see Cochrane analyses of various clinical protocols) that identified evidence-based treatments for various clinical conditions, based on rigorous literature analyses. However, once identified, one needs a detailed published clinical protocol to deliver those treatments in research, clinical practice, and/or training (see David & Montgomery, 2011). Please submit your proposal to Series Editor Daniel David: daniel.david@ubbcluj.ro.

Ioana Alina Cristea • Simona Stefan
Oana David • Cristina Mogoase
Anca Dobrean

REBT in the Treatment of Anxiety Disorders in Children and Adults

Springer

Ioana Alina Cristea
Clinical Psychology and Psychotherapy
Babes-Bolyai University
Cluj Napoca, Romania

Oana David
Clinical Psychology and Psychotherapy
Babes-Bolyai University
Cluj Napoca, Romania

Anca Dobrean
Clinical Psychology and Psychotherapy
Babes-Bolyai University
Cluj Napoca, Romania

Simona Stefan
Clinical Psychology and Psychotherapy
Babes-Bolyai University
Cluj Napoca, Romania

Cristina Mogoase
Clinical Psychology and Psychotherapy
Babes-Bolyai University
Cluj-Napoca, Romania

ISSN 2192-8363 ISSN 2192-8371 (electronic)
SpringerBriefs in Psychology
ISBN 978-3-319-18418-0 ISBN 978-3-319-18419-7 (eBook)
DOI 10.1007/978-3-319-18419-7

Library of Congress Control Number: 2015942144

Springer Cham Heidelberg New York Dordrecht London

Printed on acid-free paper

Springer International Publishing AG Switzerland is part of Springer Science+Business Media (www.springer.com)

Contents

About the Authors

Ioana Alina Cristea, Ph.D. is a Senior Assistant Professor at Department of Clinical Psychology and Psychotherapy, Babes-Bolyai University, Cluj-Napoca, and a Research Fellow at the University of Pisa, Italy. She holds a master's degree in Clinical Psychology, a Ph.D. in Psychology, and is a board certified cognitive-behavioral therapist by the Romanian National Board of Psychologists. She is also certified by the Albert Ellis Institute, New York, as a REBT psychotherapist and is a fellow of International Institute for the Advanced Studies of Psychotherapy and Applied Mental Health at Babes-Bolyai University. She is a senior editor of the *Journal of Evidence-Based Psychotherapy* (http://jebp.psychotherapy.ro). Her main research interests include evidence-based psychological interventions, critically appraising the efficiency and mechanisms of action of psychotherapy interventions, and the regulation of emotions.

Oana David, Ph.D. is Associate Professor in the Department of Clinical Psychology and Psychotherapy at Babes-Bolyai University, and director of the International Coaching Institute and European Coaching Center within the Department. She received her Ph.D. in psychology in 2011 from the Babes-Bolyai University for the thesis "Evidence-based parenting programs for child disruptive behaviors." Dr. Oana David is also a clinical psychologist and followed specializing programs in counseling psychology at King's College London, Institute of Psychiatry, UK, psychotherapy at Albert Ellis Institute, New York, and coaching at Centre for Coaching, UK. Her professional expertise includes technology-based interventions (e.g., online, virtual reality) for various populations, like children, parents, and executives.

Anca Dobrean, Ph.D. is currently Associate Professor and head of the Department of Clinical Psychology and Psychotherapy, Faculty of Psychology and Sciences of Education, Babes-Bolyai University, Romania. She is senior psychologist in clinical psychology, psychological counseling, and psychotherapy certified by the Romanian National Board of Psychologists. She is trained in cognitive therapy and rational emotive behavior therapy (REBT) and certified by the Albert Ellis Institute, New York. She is a fellow of the International Institute for the Advanced Studies of Psychotherapy and Applied Mental Health at Babes-Bolyai University. Dr. Dobrean is involved in national and international clinical trials of the efficacy of cognitive behavioral interventions in child and adolescent emotional and behavioral problems such as anxiety, ADHD, and disruptive behavior. She is currently the principal investigator for a large clinical trial on the efficacy of a web platform in the treatment of childhood anxiety.

Cristina Mogoase, Ph.D. is currently Senior Assistant Professor within Department of Clinical Psychology and Psychotherapies, Faculty of Psychology and Sciences of Education, Babes-Bolyai University, Romania. She is a clinical psychologist and cognitive-behavioral psychotherapist certified by the Romanian National Board of Psychologists. She is also certified by the Albert Ellis Institute, New York, as a REBT psychotherapist. She is a fellow of the International Institute for the Advanced Studies of Psychotherapy and Applied Mental Health at Babes-Bolyai University. Dr. Mogoase is involved in national and international clinical trials of the efficacy of cognitive behavioral interventions for emotional problems in children, adolescents, and adults.

Simona Stefan, Ph.D. is a Senior Assistant Professor at the Department of Clinical Psychology and Psychotherapy, Babes-Bolyai University, and a member of the International Institute for the Advanced Studies of Psychotherapy and Applied Mental Health. Her Ph.D. thesis focused on investigating the functional/dysfunctional nature of worry in relation to other relevant factors like anxiety or irrational beliefs, and her postdoctoral studies focused on investigating the role of worry and related psychological constructs in irritable bowel syndrome. Her main research interests are in evidence-based psychological interventions, emotion regulation, and clinical health psychology. Simona Stefan is also a clinical psychologist and psychotherapist and a member of the Romanian Association for Cognitive and Behavioral Psychotherapies. She is also currently executive director of the "Psytech" Babes-Bolyai University Clinic.

Chapter 1
General Overview

1.1 Anxiety Disorders: General Overview

Anxiety disorders are the most prevalent form of psychological disturbance, with 25–30 % lifetime prevalence rates for at least one anxiety disorder (Kessler, Chiu, Demler, & Walters, 2005). The World Health Organization (WHO) estimated that anxiety was the most common disorder in almost every country with 1-year prevalence ranging from 2.4 % in Shanghai, China, to 18.2 % in the United States (Demyttenaere et al. 2004). Anxiety is consistently related to a poorer quality of life (Olatunji, Cisler, & Tolin, 2007) and is also associated with high economic costs, due to the burden it imposes on health services—10–20 % of primary care patients actually suffering from anxiety disorders (Ansseau et al., 2004; Olfson et al., 1997, 2000). Moreover, anxiety disorders tend to become chronic, persisting long over time when untreated (Craske, 2003), while only between one third and one half of treated patients (with panic disorder, social phobia, or generalized anxiety disorder) achieve full remission (Yonkers, Bruce, Dyck, & Keller, 2003) in the course of 8 years. Along with the fact that about 50 % of anxiety disorders remain undetected in primary care (Wittchen & Boyer, 1998), and that many anxiety disorder patients do not present to primary care services (Andrews, Issakidis, & Carter, 2001), the negative consequences of anxiety disorders appear even more prominent. Also, the comorbidity rates, especially with depression and other anxiety disorders, are extremely high, being rather the norm than the exception. For example, more than half the patients diagnoses with an anxiety disorder also suffer from depressive disorders (Kessler et al., 1996), with anxiety disorders tending to precede depressive disorders temporally (Alloy, Kelly, Mineka, & Clements, 1990).

With regard to treatment, cognitive behavioral therapy (CBT) is considered the golden standard by many clinical guidelines (Chambless & Ollendick, 2001; Clark, 2011), while pharmacological treatments, especially in the form of SSRIs and benzodiazepines, have also been shown to be efficacious (Baldwin et al., 2014).

I.A. Cristea et al., *REBT in the Treatment of Anxiety Disorders in Children and Adults*, SpringerBriefs in Psychology, DOI 10.1007/978-3-319-18419-7_1

1.2 Distinguishing Normal Fear and Anxiety

As contrasted to fear, which is the psychophysiological reaction to the appraisal of *imminent* danger, the concept of anxiety refers to a more enduring emotional state related to threat or anxious apprehension in relation to a possible but not necessarily present fear-related stimulus (Barlow, 2002). While fear is a normal and adaptive response to danger and threat, excessive anxiety is impairing; in distinguishing between normal and abnormal fear responses, Clark and Beck (2010) have proposed several dimensions: (1) dysfunctional cognitions—according to the cognitive behavioral theory, abnormal anxiety results from erroneous beliefs about the appraisal of danger; (2) impaired functioning—anxiety interferes negatively with a person's social and professional functioning, limiting the range of performed activities (due to avoidance), and also due to the preferential allocation of cognitive resources to anxiety-related stimuli; (3) persistence—anxiety persists longer after confronting the feared stimulus and occurs much in advance, thus leaving the person in a constant state of apprehensive threat; (4) false alarms—anxious people often appraise benign stimuli as threatening, thus employing the fear response in non-threatening situations, as in the case of a panic attack, where normal bodily changes are interpreted as signs of a serious illness, and (5) stimulus hypersensitivity—the range of stimuli perceived as threatening is much widened in the case of anxious individuals (e.g., reacting fearfully not only to the presence of animals, but also to photos of them).

While all anxiety disorders have the shared component of fear exacerbation, they are different in terms of feared stimuli and core evaluations (e.g., people with panic disorder fear bodily sensations, and their core appraisal that death or going crazy is imminent, while people with social anxiety fear the social situations because they believe they are likely to be evaluated and scrutinized by others). However, anxiety disorders are often comorbid with one another, pure anxiety disorders being relatively rare (Brown, Di Nardo, Lehman, & Campbell, 2001), with generalized anxiety disorder and social phobia as the most common secondary anxiety disorders.

1.3 Anxiety Disorders in Children and Adolescents

Anxiety disorders refer to fears of unusual duration, intensity, content, or frequency, which lead to functional impairment (DSM-5; American Psychiatric Association, 2013). They refer to negatively affect-laden, future-oriented mood states, in which one experiences apprehension in relation to future negative events. Anxiety disorders include a variety of conditions, like separation anxiety disorder, selective mutism, panic disorder, generalized anxiety disorder, social phobia, or specific phobia. Anxiety disorders often share common symptoms and are highly comorbid with one another, between 40 and 70 % of anxious children meeting criteria for more than one disorder (Seligman & Ollendick, 2011).

When transient and moderate, anxiety is a normal childhood experience, its content varying with developmental stages, from immediate dangers to potential and anticipatory ones (Craske, 1997). For example, the fear of strong noises, strangers, the fear of being lost or being separated from attachment figures are prominent in the first years of life, while fears of imaginary characters, darkness, or social situations emerge at 4–5 years, together with the development of imaginative abilities (Ollendick, Matson, & Helsel, 1985). Once the child reaches adolescence, social fears of being criticized and scrutinized predominate. Normal fear and anxiety seem to follow a predictable pattern in accordance to the child's developmental stage, this being referred to as "the ontogenetic parade" (Marks, 1987).

Additionally, it seems to be a reciprocal relationship between children's mental and emotional development. Therefore, when children are very young, their emotional experiences are defined by their yet limited understanding of the world—children construct their theories of the world based only on their experience (Bernard, Ellis, & Terjesen, 2006). Such early formed beliefs are often implicit and act as unquestioned rules for guiding behavior, thus having a long-term influence on the child's emotional responses and behaviors. Moreover, it is difficult for children to distinguish between real and imaginary dangers and often fear safe or neutral stimuli because of their limited reasoning abilities (Grieger & Boyd, 2006). Their thinking is characterized by animism (i.e., thinking that inanimate objects have human characteristics), egocentrism (i.e., not being able to see that other people or beings may have different motivations and feelings), concreteness (i.e., giving literal interpretations to experiences, not being able to think abstractly or hypothetically), and inaccurate perceptions of size, time, and distance, thus making the experience of irrational fear more likely (Kessler, 1966). Though childhood fears are typical responses, not all children react to real or imagined dangers with extreme anxiety, and these differences in intensity, frequency, duration, and pervasiveness of anxious responses distinguish between normal fears and anxiety disorders. In contrast to normal childhood anxiety, an anxiety disorder is characterized by the presence of symptoms for several months, causing significant distress and functional impairment in relation to school, family life, and peer relations.

Anxiety disorders are highly prevalent in children and adolescents, affecting up to 20 % of this age group (Costello, Egger, & Angold, 2004), causing significant impairment in the academic field, family life, and general well-being (Marmorstein, White, Loeber, & Stouthamer-Loeber, 2010; Piacentini, Bergman, Keller, & McCracken, 2003). In contrast to externalizing behavior problems (e.g., oppositional behavior, ADHD), internalizing symptoms such as anxiety are underdiagnosed and undertreated because parents do not easily recognize the signs as problematic since they only affect the child.

Early onset of anxiety disorders not only increases the risk of maintenance, aggravation, and recurrence of anxious symptoms in adulthood, but also increases the risk of associated conditions across the lifespan. Epidemiological studies have documented sequential and simultaneous comorbidity between various anxiety disorders and a substantial continuity for typically childhood anxiety disorders (such as separation anxiety disorder) to various forms of adolescent and adult anxiety and affective disorders (Andlin-Sobocki & Wittchen, 2005). Comorbidities include mood disorders, substance abuse, high rates of smoking, and suicidality (Hill, Castellanos, & Pettit, 2011; Miller et al., 2011).

1.4 Rational-Emotive and Cognitive-Behavior Therapy

Rational Emotive Behavior Therapy (REBT) is one of the main cognitive-oriented treatment approaches in clinical psychology, belonging to the larger family of cognitive behavior therapy (CBT). It was first introduced by Albert Ellis in 1957 with the name of Rational Therapy (RT); later, in order to emphasize its focus on emotional outcomes, it was named Rational Emotive Therapy (RET, Ellis, 1962). Finally, in 1993, Ellis changed its name into REBT in order to highlight the importance of behavior change in therapy. It is an existentially oriented approach, designed to help clients change their self-defeating life philosophies into life-enhancing ones (Weinrach, 2006).

While all CBT approaches assume that cognitions are the causal mechanism of emotional responses, REBT differs from other approaches (e.g., standard CT, Beck, 1976) with respect to the types of beliefs which are considered to cause emotional reactions. In this sense, REBT specifically focuses on evaluative beliefs, and not inferential or descriptive ones, because, as the appraisal theory of emotion (Lazarus, 1991) states, an event has to be *evaluated* in order to elicit an emotional response. For example, someone could have a distorted interpretation of facts (e.g., "people don't like me"), but if this interpretation is not further negatively appraised (e.g., "It is bad/awful that people don't like me"), then it will not elicit a negative emotion. Therefore, REBT theorists say that the primary target of change in therapy should be evaluative or "hot" cognitions, and not inferential or "cold" cognitions.

REBT distinguishes between two fundamentally different evaluation/appraisal "styles": irrational and rational. Irrational evaluations are illogical, have no empirical and/or pragmatic support, hindering the person from achieving his/her goals, while the rational ones are logical, have empirical support, and/or help the person achieve his/her goals. According to REBT, the core irrational beliefs (e.g., "I must not fail and it is awful if I fail."), in interactions to various activating events (e.g., a test situation), generate automatic thoughts in the form of descriptions/inferences (e.g., "I will fail here.") that are then further processed by automatic thoughts in the form of specific irrational beliefs derived from the core irrational beliefs (e.g., "I must not fail here and it is awful if I fail here.") that than further generate symptoms.

The "ABC" model is the cornerstone of REBT (Ellis, 1994), where A stands for activating events, B stands for beliefs, and C stands for emotional, behavioral, and psychophysiological consequences. The initial ABC assessment framework was later expanded into the ABCDE model (Ellis, 1962; Ellis & Dryden, 1997), in recognition of the importance of disputation and replacing irrational beliefs with rational ones. In the ABCDE framework, A stands for undesirable life events "activating events" that can be (1) internal or external, (2) past, present, or future, (3) real or imagined. About activating events, people uphold rational or irrational beliefs (B), which result into affective, psycho-physiological, and behavioral consequences (C). Rational beliefs (RBs) lead to functional consequences, while irrational beliefs (IBs) lead to dysfunctional consequences (Ellis & Dryden, 1997). Once generated, the C can later convert to an A, triggering other rational/irrational beliefs (RBs/IBs) that will lead to other adaptive or maladaptive consequences. In order to change the dysfunctional consequences of their irrational thoughts, clients are encouraged to actively dispute (D) these beliefs and replace them with more efficient beliefs (E) (Ellis, 1962, 1994; Walen, DiGiuseppe, & Dryden, 1992).

More recently (David, 2003, 2015), the ABC model was expanded as to include unconscious information processes, both structurally (they were acquired unconsciously and cannot be made conscious, such as behaviors learned by classical conditioning) and functionally (they were acquired consciously but now function unconsciously, such as automatic associations). The expended ABC model is presented in Fig. 1.1.

There are six basic principles fundamental to the REBT theory, which emphasize the primacy of thought in the generation of dysfunctional emotions and psychopathology (Walen et al., 1992, pp. 15–16; Weinrach, 2006):

1. Cognitions are the most important proximal causes of emotions.
2. Dysfunctional thinking is a major factor leading to emotional distress.
3. Because emotional disturbance is caused by endorsing irrational beliefs, the best way to diminish distress is to change irrational thinking.
4. Irrational thinking and psychopathology are influenced by multiple factors, including both genetic and environmental influences.

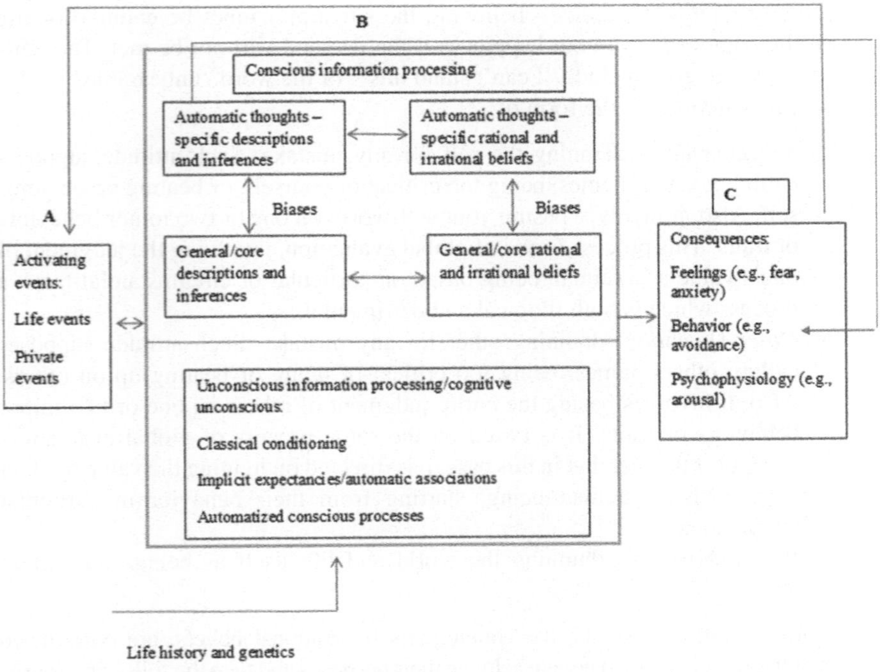

Fig. 1.1 The expanded ABC model (After David, 2015)

5. REBT emphasizes present rather than historical influences on behavior because humans maintain their disturbance through reiterated irrational thinking.
6. Beliefs can be changed, although such change will take time and will not be easy.

Irrational beliefs, as described in REBT theory, have varied over time in content and number; more recently, however, Ellis (1994) and David, Lynn, & Ellis (2010) stated that they can be subsumed to four major categories:

1. *Demands*—inflexible expectations about self, others, life. Such thoughts contain words like "must," "should," "ought," "it is fair...," "it is right...." They are rigid formulations of one's purposes and desires, stating that, if one desires *something*, that something *must* happen, and, provided it does not happen, it is unacceptable. For example, if someone holds the belief "people must like me," it means that in one's mind, people must absolutely like her, and she cannot accept it when they don't. According to the REBT theory, demands are primary irrational beliefs, all other irrational beliefs deriving from them, and they constitute the route to psychopathology.
2. *Awfulizing/Catastrophizing*—believing that a situation is more than 100 % bad, worse than it absolutely should be. These thoughts involve words like "awful," "horrible," or "terrible." When catastrophizing, people believe that a negative event which has happened or might happen to them is the worst possible thing which could have happened, and that there is no room for positive events happening again.
3. *Low Frustration Tolerance*—believing the situation cannot be endured or life will be completely without happiness if the demand will not be met. Thoughts from this category include "I can't stand this!" or the word "unbearable."
4. *Global evaluation* in the form of:

   (a) *Self-Downing*—damning the self for any mistake. Such attitude supposes calling yourself names, being too critical of yourself, or beating up on yourself. Also, it involves basing your self-worth on one or two minor behaviors or traits. This process is one of global evaluation, involving the judgment of one's value as a human being based on particular or circumstantial facts, a process which is both illogical and detrimental.
   (b) *Other-Downing*—damning other for any mistake. Such attitude supposes calling others names, being too critical of them, or beating up on others. Also, it involves basing the entire judgment of others on one or two minor behaviors or traits. It is based on the same process of global evaluation, except for the fact that in this case, it is directed on judging the value of other individuals as human being, starting from their behavior in particular circumstances.
   (c) *World-Downing*—damning the world and life itself as being bad, unfair, unjust.

Alternatively, rational beliefs, the counterparts of irrational beliefs, are constructed views of the world that help people achieve their purposes and take the following forms:

1. *Preferences*—flexible expectations about self, others, life. Such thoughts contain words like "prefer," "would like," "would be nice." Formulating one's purposes and desires in preferential terms is, however, far from indifference. They involve a strong desire to achieve one's goals, but take account of the fact that the world does not operate by one's rules, so there is always a possibility that a desired outcome does not happen.
2. *Moderate evaluations of badness*—believing that a situation is bad, but not as worse as it could be. These thoughts involve words like "bad," "unpleasant," or "unlikable." When evaluating a situation in terms of badness, the individual still sees possibilities for improvement, since the situation is not 100 % bad.
3. *High Frustration Tolerance*—believing the situation can be endured and there could be some happiness in life if one's wishes will not be met. Thoughts from this category include "I can stand this, only I don't like it."
4. *Contextual evaluation* and:

   (a) *Unconditional self-acceptance*—accepting your self is valuable in spite of occasional mistakes. Such attitude supposes believing one is a valuable human being even though sometimes his/her behaviors are not very commendable. Unconditional self-acceptance does not, however, involve accepting one's behaviors. Behaviors are good or bad, they are evaluated and they are amenable to change.
   (b) *Unconditional other-acceptance*—accepting other people are valuable in spite of occasional mistakes. Such attitude supposes believing one is valuable even though sometimes his/her behaviors are not very commendable. Similarly, other's behaviors are not unconditionally accepted; some are good and have to be enforced, while others are bad and have to be eliminated.
   (c) *Unconditional acceptance of life and the world itself*, regardless of negative and/or unjust events happening.

Rational and irrational beliefs can refer to different contents. Some are directed at oneself (e.g., "I must perform well"), others (e.g., "You must perform well"), and/or life (e.g., "Life must be just"). Additionally, they can be general (e.g., "People must like me") and/or domain-specific (e.g., affiliation, performance, comfort) and/or circumscribed to particular situations (e.g., "My wife must love me"). The specific combinations between rational and irrational processes and their content (i.e., rational and irrational beliefs) generate core themes leading to specific emotional responses. For example, "depressed mood" seems to involve a core theme of "loss" and specific irrational appraisals relating to demandingness (irrational primary appraisal) and self-downing (irrational secondary appraisal). Its functional counterpart involves the same theme of "loss," but preference (rational primary appraisal) and unconditional self/acceptance (rational secondary appraisal) as specific appraisal components (David, 2015).

When facing negative life events, irrational beliefs are associated with dysfunctional emotions, while rational beliefs are associated with functional ones (Dryden, 2002). According to the binary model of distress stemming from the REBT theory, functional and dysfunctional emotions are distinguished in terms of: (1) underlying

Table 1.1 Functional and dysfunctional emotions (After Dryden & DiGiuseppe, 1990)

Type of belief	Emotion	Functionality of emotion
Irrational	Anxiety	Dysfunctional
Rational	Concern	Functional
Irrational	Depression	Dysfunctional
Rational	Sadness	Functional
Irrational	Anger	Dysfunctional
Rational	Annoyance	Functional
Irrational	Guilt	Dysfunctional
Rational	Remorse	Functional

beliefs, with dysfunctional emotions being triggered by irrational beliefs, and functional emotions being triggered by rational beliefs; (2) their consequences, with dysfunctional emotions leading to maladaptive behavioral responses, and functional emotions (i.e., even if negative) leading to adaptive behaviors, and (3) subjective response—people experience functional and dysfunctional emotions in qualitatively different manners (David & Cramer, 2010; Ellis & DiGiuseppe, 1993). Thus, functional and dysfunctional emotions are not only different in intensity, but constitute qualitatively distinguished emotional experiences. While functional emotions, either positive or negative, constitute normal reactions to every-day life events, dysfunctional emotions correspond to subclinical and clinical problems (David & Cramer, 2010). Similarly to irrational beliefs having rational beliefs as counterparts, dysfunctional emotions have functional counterparts, the main categories being presented in Table 1.1.

The efficiency of REBT has been investigated in a series of randomized control trials, proving it efficacious for a variety of conditions like obsessive-compulsive disorder (Emmelkamp & Beens, 1991), social phobia (Mersch, Emmelkamp, Bogels, & van der Sleen, 1989), depression (David, Szentagotai, Lupu, & Cosman, 2008), side effects of breast cancer treatment (Montgomery et al., 2014; Schnur et al., 2009), psychotic symptoms (Meaden, Keen, Aston, Barton, & Bucci, 2013), parental distress (Joyce, 1995), disruptive behavior (Gaviţa, David, Bujoreanu, Tiba, & Ionuţiu, 2012), etc. Several meta-analyses have also indicated that REBT is an effective form of psychotherapy (Engels, Garnefsky, & Diekstra, 1993; Gonzalez et al., 2004; Lyons & Woods, 1991).

1.5 General Overview of the Present Book

In this book, we will present four REBT treatment protocols for anxiety disorders in adults (generalized anxiety disorder and social anxiety disorders), as well as in children and adolescents (anxiety disorders in general). Each of these has been used in a randomized controlled trial, published, submitted for publication or in preparation. Each protocol includes a therapist guide, as well as specific supplementary materials for the therapist and patients. The therapist guide includes a case formulation using the principles of REBT, as well as specific REBT techniques and a session by session guide. Supplementary materials include evaluation scales developed for session to session use, as well as patient worksheets and other exercises. The two protocols for children and adolescents also include developmentally tailored materials, like rational stories and rational cartoons. Finally, references for the therapist, as well as recommended readings for the patient are provided at the end of each chapter. The first part of the book will present two protocols for adults, and the second part, two for children and adolescents, each protocol occupying a specific chapter.

References

Alloy, L. B., Kelly, K. A., Mineka, S., & Clements, C. M. (1990). Comorbidity of anxiety and depressive disorders: A helplessness—hopelessness perspective. In J. D. Maser & C. R. Cloninger (Eds.), *Comorbidity of mood and anxiety disorders* (pp. 499–543). Washington, DC: American Psychiatric Press.

American Psychiatric Association. (2013). *Diagnostic and statistical manual of mental disorders* (5th ed.). Washington, DC: Author.

Andlin-Sobocki, P., & Wittchen, H. U. (2005). Cost of anxiety disorders in Europe. *European Journal of Neurology, 12*(s1), 39–44.

Andrews, G., Issakidis, C., & Carter, G. (2001). Shortfall in mental health service utilisation. *British Journal of Psychiatry, 179*, 417–425.

Ansseau, M., Dierick, M., Buntinkx, F., Cnockaert, P., De Smedt, J., Van Den Haute, M., et al. (2004). High prevalence of mental disorders in primary care. *Journal of Affective Disorders, 78*, 49–55.

Baldwin, D. S., Andersson, I. M., Nutt, D. J., Allgulander, C., Bandelow, B., den Boer, J. A., et al. (2014). Evidence-based pharmacological treatment of anxiety disorders, post-traumatic stress disorder and obsessive-compulsive disorder: A revision of the 2005 guidelines from the British Association for Psychopharmacology. *Journal of Psychopharmacology, 28*, 403–439.

Barlow, D. H. (2002). *Anxiety and its disorders: The nature and treatment of anxiety and panic* (2nd ed.). New York: Guilford.

Beck, A. T. (1976). *Cognitive therapy and the emotional disorders*. New York: International Universities Press.

Bernard, M., Ellis, A., & Terjesen, M. (2006). Rational emotive behavioral approaches to childhood disorders. In A. Ellis & M. Bernard (Eds.), *Rational emotive behavioral approaches to childhood disorders* (Theory, practice, and research, pp. 3–84). New York: Springer.

Brown, T. A., Di Nardo, P. A., Lehman, C. L., & Campbell, L. A. (2001). Reliability of DSM-IV anxiety and mood disorders: Implications for the classification of emotional disorders. *Journal of Abnormal Psychology, 110*, 49–58.

Chambless, D. L., & Ollendick, T. H. (2001). Empirically supported psychological interventions: Controversies and evidence. *Annual Review of Psychology, 52*, 685–716.

Clark, D. M. (2011). Implementing NICE guidelines for the psychological treatment of depression and anxiety disorders: The IAPT experience. *International Review of Psychiatry, 23*(4), 318–327.

Clark, D. A., & Beck, A. T. (2010). *Cognitive therapy of anxiety disorders: Science and practice*. New York: Guilford.

Costello, E. J., Egger, H. L., & Angold, A. (2004). The developmental epidemiology of anxiety disorders. In T. Ollendick & J. March (Eds.), *Phobic and anxiety disorders in children and adolescents* (pp. 61–91). New York: Oxford University Press.

Craske, M. G. (1997). Panic and anxiety in children and adolescent. *Supplement to the Bulletin of the Menninger Clinic, 61*, A4–A36.
Craske, M. G. (2003). *Origins of phobias and anxiety disorders: Why more women than men?* Amsterdam, The Netherlands: Elsevier.
David, D. (2003). Rational emotive behavior therapy (REBT): The view of a cognitive psychologist. In W. Dryden (Ed.), *Theoretical developments in REBT*. London: Brunner/Routledge.
David, D. (2015). Rational emotive behavior therapy. In R. L. Cautin & S. O. Lilienfeld (Eds.), *Encyclopedia of clinical psychology*. Hoboken, NJ: Wiley-Blackwell.
David, D., & Cramer, D. (2010). Rational and irrational beliefs in human feelings and psychophysiology. In D. David, S. J. Lynn, & A. Ellis (Eds.), *Rational and irrational beliefs in human functioning and disturbances*. Oxford, England: Oxford University Press.
David, D., Lynn, S.J., & Ellis, A. (2010). *Rational and irrational beliefs in human functioning and disturbances*. Oxford, England: Oxford University Press.
David, D., Szentagotai, A., Lupu, V., & Cosman, D. (2008). Rational emotive behavior therapy, cognitive therapy, and medication in the treatment of major depressive disorder: A randomized clinical trial, posttreatment outcomes, and six-month follow-up. *Journal of Clinical Psychology, 64*, 728–746.
Demyttenaere, K., Bruffaerts, R., Posada-Villa, J., Gasquet, I., Kovess, V., et al. (2004). Prevalence, severity, and unmet need for treatment of mental disorders in the World Health Organization World Mental Health Surveys. *JAMA, 291*(21), 2581–2590.
Dryden, W. (2002). *Fundamentals of rational emotive behavior therapy*. London: Whurr.
Dryden, W., & DiGiuseppe, R. (1990). *A primer on rational-emotive therapy*. Champaign, IL: Research Press.
Ellis, A. (1957). Rational psychotherapy and individual psychology. *The Journal of Individual Psychology, 13*, 38–44.
Ellis, A. (1962). *Reason and emotion in psychotherapy*. New York: Lyle Stuart.
Ellis, A. (1994). *Reason and emotion in psychotherapy* (rev. ed.). Secaucus, NJ: Birch Lane.
Ellis, A., & DiGiuseppe, R. (1993). Are inappropriate or dysfunctional feelings in rational-emotive therapy qualitative or quantitative? *Cognitive Therapy and Research, 17*, 471–477.
Ellis, A., & Dryden, W. (1997). *The practice of rational emotive behavior therapy*. New York: Springer.
Emmelkamp, P. M., & Beens, H. (1991). Cognitive therapy with obsessive-compulsive disorder: A comparative evaluation. *Behaviour Research and Therapy, 29*(3), 293–300.
Engels, G. I., Garnefsky, N., & Diekstra, R. F. (1993). Efficacy of rational-emotive therapy: A quantitative analysis. *Journal of Consulting and Clinical Psychology, 61*, 1083–1090.
Gaviţa, O. A., David, D., Bujoreanu, S., Tiba, A., & Ionuţiu, D. (2012). The efficacy of a short cognitive-behavioral parent program in the treatment of externalizing behavior disorders in Romanian foster care children: Building parental emotion-regulation through unconditional self- and child-acceptance strategies. *Children and Youth Services Review, 34*, 1290–1297.
Gonzalez, J. E., Nelson, J. R., Gutkin, T. B., Saunders, A., Galloway, A., & Shwery, C. S. (2004). Rational emotive therapy with children and adolescents: A meta-analysis. *Journal of Emotional and Behavioral Disorders, 12*, 222–235.
Grieger, R. M., & Boyd, J. D. (2006). Childhood anxieties, fears, and phobias: A cognitive-behavioral, psychosocial approach. In A. Ellis & M. Bernard (Eds.), *Rational emotive behavioral approaches to childhood disorders* (Theory, practice, and research, pp. 232–256). New York: Springer.
Hill, R. M., Castellanos, D., & Pettit, J. W. (2011). Suicide-related behaviors and anxiety in children and adolescence: A review. *Clinical Psychology Review, 31*(7), 1133–1144.
Joyce, M. R. (1995). Emotional relief for parents: Is rational-emotive parent education effective? *Journal of Rational-Emotive and Cognitive-Behavior Therapy, 13*, 55–75.
Kessler, J. (1966). *Psychopathology of childhood*. Englewood Cliffs, NJ: Prentice-Hall.
Kessler, R. C., Chiu, W. T., Demler, O., & Walters, E. E. (2005). Prevalence, severity, and comorbidity of 12-month DSM-IV disorders in the National Comorbidity Survey Replication. *Archives of General Psychiatry, 62*, 617–627.

Kessler, R. C., Nelson, C. B., McGonagle, K. A., Liu, J., Swartz, M., & Blazer, D. G. (1996). Comorbidity of DSM-III-R major depressive disorder in the general population: Results from the US National Comorbidity Survey. *British Journal of Psychiatry, 168*(Suppl. 30), 17–30.

Lazarus, R. S. (1991). *Emotion and adaptation*. New York: Oxford University Press.

Lyons, L. C., & Woods, P. J. (1991). The efficacy of rational-emotive therapy: A quantitative review of the outcome research. *Clinical Psychology Review, 11*, 357–369.

Marks, I. M. (1987). The development of normal fear: A review. *Journal of Child Psychology and Psychiatry, 28*, 667–697.

Marmorstein, N. R., White, H. R., Loeber, R., & Stouthamer-Loeber, M. (2010). Anxiety as a predictor of age at first use of substances and progression to substance use problems among boys. *Journal of Abnormal Child Psychology, 38*(2), 211–224.

Meaden, A., Keen, N., Aston, R., Barton, K., & Bucci, S. (2013). *Cognitive therapy for command hallucinations*. London: Routledge.

Mersch, P. P., Emmelkamp, P. M., Bogels, S. M., & van der Sleen, J. (1989). Social phobia: Individual response patterns and the effects of behavioral and cognitive interventions. *Behaviour Research and Therapy, 27*, 421–434.

Miller, L. D., Laye-Gindhu, A., Liu, Y., March, J. S., Thordarson, D. S., & Garland, E. J. (2011). Evaluation of a preventive intervention for child anxiety in two randomized attention control school trials. *Behaviour Research and Therapy, 49*(5), 315–323.

Montgomery, G. H., David, D., Kangas, M., Green, S., Sucala, M., Bovbjerg, D. H., et al. (2014). A randomized clinical trial of a cognitive-behavioral therapy plus hypnosis intervention to control fatigue in breast cancer radiotherapy patients. *Journal of Clinical Oncology, 32*(6), 557–563.

Olatunji, B. O., Cisler, J. M., & Tolin, D. F. (2007). Quality of life in the anxiety disorders: A meta-analytic review. *Clinical Psychology Review, 27*, 572–581.

Olfson, M., Fireman, B., Weissman, M. M., Leo, A. C., Sheehan, D. V., Kathol, R., et al. (1997). Mental disorders and disability among patients in a primary care group practice. *American Journal of Psychiatry, 154*, 1734–1740.

Olfson, M., Shea, S., Feder, A., Fuentes, M., Nomura, Y., Gameroff, M., et al. (2000). Prevalence of anxiety, depression and substance use disorders in an urban general medicine practice. *Archives of Family Medicine, 9*, 876–883.

Ollendick, T. H., Matson, J. L., & Helsel, W. J. (1985). Fears in children and adolescents: Normative data. *Behaviour Research and Therapy, 23*, 465–467.

Piacentini, J., Bergman, R. L., Keller, M., & McCracken, J. (2003). Functional impairment of children and adolescents with obsessive-compulsive disorder. *Journal of Child and Adolescent Psychopharmacology, 13*(s1), 61–69.

Schnur, J. B., David, D., Kangas, M., Green, S., Bovbjerg, D. M., & Montgomery, G. M. (2009). A randomized trial of a cognitive-behavioral therapy and hypnosis intervention on positive and negative affect during breast cancer radiotherapy. *Journal of Clinical Psychology, 65*, 443–455.

Seligman, L. D., & Ollendick, T. H. (2011). Cognitive behavioral therapy for anxiety disorders in youth. *Child and Adolescent Psychiatric Clinics of North America, 20*(2), 217–238.

Walen, S. R., DiGiuseppe, R., & Dryden, W. (1992). *A practitioner's guide to rational-emotive therapy* (2nd ed.). New York: Oxford University Press.

Weinrach, S. G. (2006). Nine experts describe the essence of rational-emotive therapy while standing on one foot. *Journal of Rational-Emotive & Cognitive-Behavior Therapy, 24*, 217–232.

Wittchen, H.-U., & Boyer, P. (1998). Screening for anxiety disorders: Sensitivity and specificity of the Anxiety Screening Questionnaire (ASQ-15). *British Journal of Psychiatry, 173*(Suppl. 34), 10–17.

Yonkers, K. A., Bruce, S. E., Dyck, I. R., & Keller, M. B. (2003). Chronicity, relapse, and illness: Course of panic disorder, social phobia, and generalized anxiety disorder. Findings in men and women from 8 years of follow-up. *Depression and Anxiety, 17*, 173–179.

Part I
Treatment of Anxiety Disorders in Adults

Chapter 2
Rational-Emotive and Cognitive-Behavior Therapy for Generalized Anxiety Disorder

2.1 Generalized Anxiety Disorder

Generalized anxiety disorder (GAD) is defined by the experience of pervasive and uncontrollable worry, in combination with other symptoms related to prolonged physical arousal, like restlessness, irritability, or difficulty sleeping (DSM-5, American Psychiatric Association, 2000). Worry, the core diagnosis feature of GAD, refers to "a chain of thoughts and images, negatively affect-laden and relatively uncontrollable" (Borkovec, Robinson, Pruzinsky, & DePree, 1983, p. 10), with reference to a wide range of domains, like health, financial status, education, family, and so on. While mild and transient worry is a common process in normal population, pathological worry is experienced as pervasive, uncontrollable, and dangerous (Holaway, Heimberg, & Coles, 2006).

GAD is a highly prevalent, chronic, and debilitating mental condition, with prevalence rates ranging between 1.2 and 1.9 for 12 months prevalence, and 4.3 % and 5.9 % for lifetime prevalence, respectively (Tyrer & Baldwin, 2006), being also associated with significant distress and impairment (Kessler, Walters, & Wittchen, 2004). GAD is a chronic disorder, in many cases lasting for a decade or longer (Kessler & Wittchen, 2002), and with low rates of spontaneous remission (Brown, Barlow, & Liebowitz, 1994; Wittchen & Hoyer, 2001). In clinical and community studies, GAD emerges as a strong predictor of functional impairment, over and above that functional impairment explained by major depression (Stein, 2004). With reference to comorbidity, data show that pure GAD cases are relatively rare, with approximately 60–90 % of patients meeting criteria for another disorder (e.g., Brown, Barlow, & Liebowitz, 1994). However, the high comorbidity rate could also be biased since individuals with pure GAD seldom seek medical or psychological support (Heimberg, Turk, & Mennin, 2004).

The most studied CBT model for GAD is Borkovec's cognitive avoidance model (CAM; Borkovec & Costello, 1993). The model revolves around the concept of worry as a verbal attempt to problem-solve possible future negative events, with the

I.A. Cristea et al., *REBT in the Treatment of Anxiety Disorders in Children and Adults*, SpringerBriefs in Psychology, DOI 10.1007/978-3-319-18419-7_2

goal of reducing or inhibiting aversive mental imagery, emotional experience, and bodily sensations (see Sibrava & Borkovec, 2006 for a review of the model). Consequently, worry becomes self-reinforcing. As a therapeutical approach, it includes applied relaxation (AR; Ost, 1987) that is carried out during anxiety inducing, worry connected, mental imagery, as well as traditional cognitive therapy methods (e.g., identification and disputation of dysfunctional thoughts, generating alternative and more accurate thoughts, behavioral experiments) as described by Beck and Emery (1985). However, other more recent theoretical and therapeutical models of GAD exist, such as the intolerance of uncertainty model (IUM; Ladouceur et al., 2000), the metacognitive model (MCM; Wells & King, 2006), or acceptance-based behavior therapy (ABBT; Roemer & Orsillo, 2005).

2.2 Key Elements of the REBT Intervention for GAD: A Therapist Guide

The chapter further presents an REBT protocol designed for treating GAD. The protocol has been tested in a randomized control trial, comparing its efficacy with standard cognitive therapy (CT) and Acceptance and Commitment Therapy (ACT). The results show no significant differences among treatment arms, thus supporting the efficacy of REBT in treating GAD (Cristea et al., submitted).

We will subsequently present the REBT protocol used in a randomized control trial for GAD, a study comparing REBT with cognitive therapy—Borkovec's treatment package (CT/BTP, Sibrava & Borkovec, 2006) and a form of ACT—acceptance-based behavior therapy (ACT/ABBT, Roemer & Orsillo, 2005), respectively. The protocol is based on Dryden and DiGiuseppe (1990). *A Primer on Rational-Emotive Therapy. Champaign, IL: Research Press (for research purposes) and David, D., Kangas, M., Schnur, J.B., and Montgomery, G.H. (2004). REBT depression manual; Managing depression using rational emotive behavior therapy. Babes-Bolyai University (BBU), Romania.*

Participants ($N=53$) were recruited starting with 2010–2014, through specialized mental health services. All participants were diagnosed with GAD as their primary diagnosis following the DSM-IV, by using the Structured Clinical Interview for DSM IV (SCID; First, Spitzer, Gibbon, & Williams, 1996). The participants were aged between 21 and 50 ($m=26.64$, SD$=6.65$), 46 were females and 7 were males. Our exclusion criteria were: severe major depression, bipolar disorder, panic disorder, substance use/abuse/dependence, psychotic disorders, suicidal or homicidal ideation, organic brain syndrome, disabling medical conditions, mental retardation, concurrent treatment with psychotropic drug, and/or psychotherapy outside study. Patients with comorbid anxiety disorder diagnoses (e.g., social phobia, specific phobia) were recruited in the trial provided their primary diagnosis was GAD, but we excluded patients with panic disorder because the focus of treatment for this condition is substantially different. In the REBT group, 17 participants received allocated intervention, ten completing all measures at post-test. In order to test the efficacy of the three treatment approaches, we measure worry and generalized anxiety symptoms as primary outcomes, and negative automatic thoughts as secondary outcomes, using widely acknowledged instruments:

2.2.1 Primary Outcomes and Secondary Outcomes

GAD Questionnaire IV (GAD-Q-IV; Newman et al., 2002)—a 9-item self-report measuring the DSM-IV criteria for GAD. The GAD-Q-IV was designed as a screening tool for GAD, and it can be scored both in a dimensional and in a categorical manner. Penn State Worry Questionnaire (PSWQ; Meyer, Miller, Metzger, & Borkovec, 1990)—a 16-item instrument designed to measure trait worry in terms of frequency and controllability.

Automatic Thoughts Questionnaire (ATQ; Hollon & Kendall, 1980)—a 15-item measure of negative automatic thoughts, typically related to many stressful experiences (e.g., depressed mood, anxious symptoms).

The results indicated that all three CBT forms (i.e., CT/BTP, REBT, and ACT/ABBT) were similarly effective in reducing generalized anxiety symptoms and worry—the key symptom of GAD, measured with both instruments: GAD-Q-IV and PSWQ. Also, all three treatments decreased both frequency and believability of dysfunctional automatic thoughts from pre to post-treatment.

2.2.2 Treatment Goals

The intervention begins with explaining the basic rules of therapy (scheduling, confidentiality, importance of homework, etc.), the rationale of REBT, the ADCDE model, and the goals of REBT to the patient. Given the particularities of GAD, the REBT approach aims to meet the following goals:

1. (a) Focus on reducing secondary disturbances (anxiety about anxiety); (b) focusing on changing specific irrational beliefs; (c) focusing on changing general irrational beliefs, (d) focusing on reducing physiological arousal, (e) focusing on reducing phobic avoidance.
2. Conceptualize the patients' problems using the ABCDE model.
3. Use of cognitive, behavioral, and emotive techniques to change the irrational beliefs into rational beliefs.
4. Use of homework assignments focused on changing irrational thinking and implement adaptive behaviors.

The REBT treatment is focused on the irrational beliefs mediating anxiety symptoms: demandingness (DEM), awfulizing (AWF), low frustration tolerance (LFT), and self-downing (SD). Intervention targets specifically (1) reducing secondary emotional problems (emotions-related emotions, such as anxiety about anxiety), (2) finding and changing DEM as the central irrational belief, (3) finding and changing AWF as a specific irrational belief involved in anxiety, and (4) fostering unconditional self-acceptance as a way of relapse prevention and promote mental health.

Frequently in REBT, the central irrational belief (i.e., DEM) is not readily recognizable (in homework or assessment instruments); in such instances, the therapist either uses inferential chaining to go from inferences to evaluations, or infers its presence from its derivatives (i.e., AWF, LFT, SD). However, the disputation of inferred DEM is made only if the patient accepts the clinical conceptualization including DEM. Although the automatic thoughts and faulty inferences are not the main focus of interventions in REBT, they will be approached, if necessary, shortly after changing the irrational evaluations.

A wide array of cognitive, behavioral, and emotive techniques will be used to change the target irrational beliefs.

2.2.3 *Session by Session Structure*

The REBT intervention consists of 20 individual 50-min therapy sessions. Therapy sessions are highly structured. They start by setting an agenda, which lists items to be dealt with during the session. Patient and therapist agree on the contents of the agenda. It always includes a review of the previous week's homework and then covers one or two specific problems, which will be the main focus of the session. Sessions end with setting a homework assignment which follows up a topic discussed during the session. Sessions should therefore follow the following format (Beck, 1995a):

- Brief Update and Mood Check
- Bridge from Previous Session
- Set Agenda
- Review Homework
- Potential supporting exercises (see below)
- Summary
- Assign Homework
- Feedback

2.2.3.1 The Initial Phase

Weeks 1–4 are included in the initial phase. In order to implement rapid symptom change, in this stage, the sessions are held bi-weekly. Sessions 1–2 (depending on the specifics of the case and patient characteristics) target the following introductory elements:

- **Clinical diagnosis and assessment**; in this stage the diagnosis was established according to the DSM criteria, by using the SCID (First et al., 1996), and participants were also asked to complete measures of symptoms (e.g., GADQ-IV, PSWQ) and also hypothesized causal mechanisms such as irrational beliefs (e.g., ABS II, DiGiuseppe, Leaf, Exner, & Robin, 1988). Measuring symptoms and cognitive mediating mechanisms is important in clinical practice even if the intervention is a not a part of an RCT because (1) we can have an objective measure of the patient's progress throughout the treatment, (2) we know which particular cognitions are likely to be problematic so we can target them more precisely, and (3) we the patient can track his progress if we present these information in a visual graphic format.

- **Commencing the construction of the therapeutic relationship**; in REBT, the therapeutic relationship is similar to CBT in general, being characterized by empathy, unconditional acceptance, congruence, collaboration—with a shared perspective on treatment expectancies, agenda, conceptualization and treatment goals, and the causes for psychological distress (Alford & Beck, 1997). Compared to other CBT approaches, REBT therapists are often seen as more active and directive; however, there are wide variations among therapists and therapists' style is also modeled according to patient characteristics (e.g., some patients respond better to directive approaches, respond to a format/informal style, prefer humor or not, etc., Dryden & Neenan, 2006).
- **Education for psychotherapy and REBT** (emphasizing the importance of homework and taking responsibility for change); it is important to share with patients that REBT is an active, short-term form of therapy, requiring their full commitment. Even from the beginning we need to emphasize that the goal of REBT is changing irrational thinking into rational thinking, and this requires forming new mental habits. As existing irrational beliefs have become the habitual response to negative events, it takes exercise to respond with rational beliefs; like all newly acquired skills, this requires practice, in the form of completing homework assignments.
- **Adjusting treatment expectations**; it is important to build hope with regard to treatment success, telling patients that they can learn new skills for dealing with problematic emotions and behaviors. However, we have to remain realistic; we know from the filed literature that CBT has generally a 6-months follow-up response rate of 50 % with GAD (Fisher & Durham, 1999), and even less with long-term follow-up, only 30–40 % being considered recovered (Durham, Chambers, MacDonald, Power, & Major, 2003), so we have to remain cautious.
- **Elaborating the problem list**; every nosological diagnosis can be translated into specific life problems for each patient. For example, with GAD, one patient could be more worried in relation to health and hazards, while another might be more concerned with performance, finances, and approval. Additionally, they may have different maladaptive-associated behaviors (e.g., avoiding negative stimuli such as TV news or sad movies versus avoiding challenging, uncertain situations). So, we will list with the patient his/her personalized problem list and then address them in turn in therapy. It is recommended for the list to include 6–8 problems; if it is too long, it can be discouraging, and, in this case, we can group problems into larger categories (e.g., communication problems with the husband,

the children, and the siblings could be grouped in a category of "family communication problems").

- **General conceptualization of GAD**. REBT does not introduce specific explanatory models for each disorder, as the core cognitive mechanisms (i.e., irrational beliefs) are considered to be transdiagnostic. Traditional CBT has so far promoted specific models for each disorder (e.g., avoidance model of worry and GAD, meta-cognitive model, and so on); however, more recently, the focus on transdiagnostic features of mental disorders has increased (e.g., Beck & Haigh, 2014). Given that irrational beliefs can be focused on various contents, it follows that in anxiety disorders, irrational beliefs related to the themes of "threat" and "uncertainty" will lead to dysfunctional emotions (i.e., anxiety). Apart from demands, which are generally primary appraisals, awfulizing/catasprophizing appears to be particularly relevant for GAD, possible leading to worry precisely due to the overestimation of negative consequences in the event of a negative outcome happening.

Homework Suggestions

- Self-monitoring of anxiety symptoms; this can be done by completing daily ABCDE forms, as exemplified in the patient guideline.
- Monitoring of previous coping strategies with anxiety—for example, keeping a diary of safety behaviors (e.g., avoiding the news, reassurance seeking).

2.2.3.2 Sessions 2–8

After introducing the patient to the REBT model in the initial phase, the therapist addresses the problems identified in the problem list in turn, by using the ABCDE model. In this sense, the therapist works toward strengthening the patients' rational beliefs and weakening the irrational beliefs by using techniques such as rational disputation, metaphors, stories, humor, and so on. In this phase, it is also very important to encourage the patients to see the links between problems, particularly those which are characterized by common irrational beliefs. At this stage, patients should also be taught a relaxation exercise, like autogenous training or applied relaxation, in order to deal with their constant state of increased arousal.

Homework Suggestions

- Emotion control by cognitive restructuring when prone to phobic avoidance
- Self-monitoring while using cognitive restructuring techniques in imagined situations
- Self-monitoring while using cognitive restructuring techniques in real life situations
- Rehearsal of relaxation exercises

2.2.3.3 Middle Phase: Weeks 5–8 (One Session Each per Week)

The middle phase of treatment includes sessions 9–16. Main goals during this stage refer to: (1) Working toward strengthening the patients' adaptive beliefs and weakening the maladaptive beliefs, thus continuing the work initiated previously; and (2) Encourage the patients to see the links between problems, particularly those which are characterized by common irrational beliefs, thus aiming to change core beliefs. At this stage, the patients should be able to recognize problematic trigger situations and use rational thinking in order to deal with them. For this purpose, patients should, by this time, know what their cognitive vulnerabilities (e.g., self-downing beliefs in relation to performance) are and try to deal with them either in advance of a difficult situation (e.g., prior to a job interview), and/or replace irrational thoughts with rational ones when anxiety appears (e.g., replacing thoughts such as "I am worthless if I fail" with rational ones, like "I accept myself as a imperfect human being whether I fail or not")

Homework Suggestions

- Rehearsing rational statements in real life situations.
- Use the cognitive conceptualization (ABCDE model) to deal with negative emotions.

2.2.3.4 The Final Phase: Weeks 9–12 (One Session Each Week)

Sessions 17–20 should be focused on (1) preparing patients for the task of becoming his/her own future therapist; and (2) discuss dependency problems and relapse prevention. The ability of using rational thinking in difficult situations should be further exercised, and patients should be trained to recognize the signs of relapse in case in occurs (e.g., persistent and frequent worry, increased psychophysiological arousal). Some patients may have difficulty believing they can deal with their emotional problems without the help of the therapist; so, previously learned strategies should be rehearsed while discussing possible future problematic situations.

Homework Suggestions

- Continuous use of the self-control techniques in real-life situations.

2.3 REBT Intervention for GAD: A Patient Guide

We will further introduce the REBT patient manual we designed for patients, based on Dryden & DiGiuseppe (1990) and David, Kangas, Schnur, & Montgomery (2004). We will also provide a list of useful readings for patients.

2.3.1 Aim of the REBT Anxiety Manual

The aim of this manual is to teach you a variety of skills and to help you manage any anxiety symptoms or anxiety-related problems you might experience.

2.3.2 Definitions

(a) What is Generalized Anxiety Disorder (GAD)?
In everyday life, moderate levels of apprehension and fear are considered to be normal, justified by some of the most stressful life events. However, anxiety disorders are not merely elevated levels of normal fear. The concept of "anxiety" refers to a combination of thoughts, emotions, behaviors, and psychophysiological reactions that cause distress and dysfunctionality. At the cognitive level, anxiety is characterized by inflexibility and a tendency to worry about everything and to evaluate events catastrophically. At the subjective level, the main emotions experienced are concern, preoccupation, intense fear, and sometimes even panic. The behavioral level is dominated by avoidance behaviors (e.g., avoiding negative information, like the news, or avoiding situations such as travels, driving, unfamiliar places, because of uncertainty and worry), while at the physiological level occur bodily reactions like accelerated heart rate, muscle tension, sweating, trembling, shortness of breath, chest pain or discomfort, nausea, chills or hot flushes, etc. These specific symptoms and the fear of these symptoms are disabling and, as a consequence, successful treatment strategies will address all these dimensions.[1]

Anxiety disorders cause considerable distress and are often chronic in nature. Persons suffering from anxiety disorders often recognize the irrational and intrusive character of their fears and seek help for them. According to the DSM-IV-TR GAD is one subtype of anxiety disorder, the broader category also including disorders like:

- Panic disorder (with or without agoraphobia)—multiple panic attacks, followed by the fear of them reoccurring and possible avoidance of context in which they might reappear (e.g., crowded places).
- Agoraphobia without history of panic disorder.
- Acute stress disorder—anxiety due to a traumatic event after it occurred (e.g., a car accident).
- Post-traumatic stress disorder—the painful relieving of traumatic memories (e.g., in the form of nightmares, flashbacks) related to a traumatic event in the past, accompanied by high anxiety.
- Obsessive-compulsive disorder—holding intrusive thoughts which seem uncontrollable despite multiple attempts to control them (e.g., contamination

[1]For further reading, visit http://gad.about.com.

fears, thoughts that one could harm another without intent) and/or compulsive behaviors (e.g., excessive washing, checking, counting).
- Specific phobias—excessive fear of specific situations (e.g., elevators, heights), animals, natural phenomena.
- Social phobia (social anxiety disorder)—fear of being scrutinized or negatively evaluated by others.

DSM-IV-TR (Diagnostic and Statistical Manual of Mental Disorders, fourth edition, revised), published by the American Psychiatric Association, states that "the essential feature of GAD is excessive anxiety and worry (apprehensive expectation), occurring more days than not for a period of at least 6 months, about a number of events or activities." Further, "the individual finds it difficult to control the worry. The anxiety and worry are accompanied by at least three additional symptoms from a list that includes restlessness, being easily fatigued, difficulty concentrating, irritability, muscle tension, and disturbed sleep.

The focus of the anxiety and worry is not confined to features of another disorder (e.g., being embarrassed in public, having panic attacks, being contaminated, being away from home etc.)." The description of GAD in DSM-IV-TR continues by stating that "although individuals with GAD may not always identify the worries as excessive, they report subjective distress due to constant worry, have difficulty controlling the worry, or experience related impairment in social, occupational or other important areas of functioning." GAD frequently co-occurs with mood disorders (e.g., depression, dysthymic disorder), other anxiety disorders (e.g., panic disorder, social phobia, and specific phobias), substance-related disorders, and other conditions like irritable bowel syndrome and headaches.

Anxiety disorders can develop at all ages, yet some forms of anxiety are more common at a certain developmental stage than others. For example, separation anxiety is more frequent in children, while social anxiety is more common in adolescents. Although most of the persons diagnosed with GAD experience early symptoms beginning in childhood and adolescence, the onset of the disorder can occur at any age. The course of the condition is chronic; there are, however, intensifications during stressful periods.

The impact of GAD can be considerable for the individual in terms of economic well-being and health and also on the society in terms of sickness and absence from work, labor turnover, and reduced productivity.

2.3.3 *What Is REBT?*

Rational Emotive Behavior Therapy (REBT) is the first form of cognitive behavior therapy (CBT) and was created by Dr. Albert Ellis. According to the REBT model, people experience undesirable activating events, about which they have rational beliefs (RBs) and irrational beliefs (IBs). These beliefs then lead to emotional, behavioral, and cognitive consequences. Rational beliefs lead to functional consequences, while irrational beliefs lead to dysfunctional consequences. Clients who engage in

REBT are encouraged to actively dispute their IBs and to assimilate more efficient, adaptive, and rational beliefs, with a positive impact on their emotional, cognitive, and behavioral responses (Ellis, 1962, 1994; Walen et al., 1992). Thus, REBT is a psychological theory and a treatment consisting of a combination of three different types of techniques (cognitive, behavioral, and emotive) you can use to help yourself feel better physically and emotionally, and to engage in healthier behaviors.

2.3.4 Managing Anxiety with Cognitive Techniques: The Power of Our Thoughts

- Although we may not always be aware of our thoughts, they nevertheless can have a strong effect on how we feel and behave in response to a particular situation or event.

  (a) Re-learning our A-B-Cs:

  - According to the cognitive theory, the effect that our thoughts can have on our physical, behavioral, and emotional responses to a particular situation can be illustrated using the following diagram:

    A = **A**ctivating event or situation that we experience

    ↓

    B = **B**eliefs or thoughts regarding the situation

    ↓

    C = **C**onsequence: How we feel or act based on these beliefs

  (b) How to think in a more rational way—The alphabet approach (A-B-C-D-E-F):

  Let's Start at the Very Beginning: A's (Activating Events)

  - On the top of the form (the ABC monitoring form, see page 37), on the left hand side, you will see a box labeled "A (Activating Events)."
  - In this box, we would like you to write about an upsetting event that happened to you today. We have provided some examples of upsetting events below the box, but you should fill in examples that are personal to you.
  - We would like to particularly encourage you to focus on monitoring the times when you feel particularly sad or when you are anxious/worried.
  - If there is a day where nothing particularly upsetting happens, we would like you to fill in this "A" box with either (a) an upsetting event that happened to you in the past, or (b) an upsetting event you've made up.

    EXAMPLE: "I feel worried because of my insecure life, and wonder how I am going to get through the rest of the day".

  Before we move on to B's, let's first focus on C's.

  C's: Consequences Following the Events

  - On the top of the form, on the right hand side, you will see a box labeled "C (Consequences)."

- In this box, we would like you to write the consequences of the event.
- There can be three types of consequences. You may experience one, two, or all three of them:

  Unhealthy negative feelings. Below the box, we have included a few examples of unhealthy negative feelings (e.g., anxiety, fear, rage). However, we encourage you to write in whatever words best describe your experience.

  Unhelpful behaviors. Below the box, we have included some examples of unhelpful behaviors. These are things you do that are unproductive or harmful in some way.

  Negative Physical Consequences of Distress. When people experience an upsetting event, they may experience some physical symptoms. For example, if you argue with a friend, you may find yourself flushed, hot, or shaking. We have listed some examples of physical consequences below the box, but again, please write any physical reactions you experience.

The Keys to Change: B's (Negative or Unhelpful Beliefs)

- As we have shown above, even though it may seem like an upsetting event (A) leads you to feel upset (C), this is not 100 % true.
- In reality, it is not the event itself that upsets you, it is your negative or unhelpful beliefs (B's) about the event that upset you.
- So how do you identify your negative or unhelpful beliefs?
- See if your beliefs fall into any of the following categories:

  - ***Demands***—Check to see if your thoughts contain the words "must," "should," or "ought." For example, you might think, "I **must** be able to do all of my errands today!" or, you might think "Life **should** be fair."
  - ***Awfulizing/Catastrophizing***—Check to see if your thoughts involve words like "awful," "horrible," or "terrible." For example, you might think, "I was too worried to leave the house, and that's **AWFUL**! I'm usually active all day long."
  - ***Frustration Intolerance***—Check to see if your thoughts include "I can't stand this!" or the word "unbearable." For example, you might think, "I **can't stand** being worried like this!"
  - ***Self-Downing***—Check to see if you're calling yourself names, being too critical of yourself, or beating up on yourself. Also, check to see if you're basing your self-worth on one or two minor things. For example, you might think, "I was too tense to make dinner for my kids today. **I'm an insensitive mother and a terrible person**."
  - ***Other-Downing***—Check to see if you're being too critical of or beating up on others, or basing your entire judgment of them on one or two minor things. For example, you might think, "My husband isn't very good at talking with me about my anxieties. **He's totally insensitive and useless**."
  - ***Life-Downing***—Check to see if you're judging *all* of your life as bad, just because it's not perfect. For example, you might think "Life is worthless because I feel so worn out."

Remember, *negative thoughts* are those thoughts that make us feel and/or behave in a negative, hurtful, or unpleasant manner (e.g., feeling anxious, or angry and being short-tempered). Once you recognize the negative belief you have about the situation, please write it in the "B" box.

D's: Debating Your Negative Beliefs

- After you recognize your negative or unhelpful thoughts, the next step is to **DEBATE** or challenge them. There are lots of different ways you can do this.
- First, you can ask yourself, "Where is holding this belief getting me? Is it helpful, or is it getting me into trouble?"
  - For example, if your belief leads you to feel upset (e.g., to cry, to feel anxious), to do things that are unhelpful or harmful to you (e.g., stop socializing with friends, not following through on treatment recommendations), or to physically feel worse (e.g., to feel more anxious), then you might decide that your belief is unhelpful.
- Second, you can ask yourself, "Where is the evidence to support my negative belief? Is it logical?"
  - For example, I may think, "I CAN'T STAND feeling so tense." But if I stop, and really consider this, I realize I can stand it. I'm still waking up every morning, I'm still taking care of my medical appointments, etc. So even though I may not like feeling so tense, I can stand it.
- Please write in box D what you said to yourself to debate and dispute your negative thoughts.

E's: Effective/Helpful Beliefs

- Once you have successfully debated against your negative beliefs, you are ready to replace them with new more effective or more helpful beliefs.
- Healthier beliefs may sound like one of the following:
  - ***Preferences***—These are a healthier, more rational alternative to demands. Preferences are when you wish for something, or want it very badly, but do not demand that it must be so. For example, you might think, "I really wish I had the energy I used to have," instead of saying, "I MUST feel exactly the way I did before I got anxiety."
  - ***Anti-Awfulizing***—This is a healthier, more rational alternative to awfulizing. This is when you can recognize that a situation is very bad, without thinking it is 100 % AWFUL. For example, you might think, "Being too worried to go to work 5 days a week is really bad, but at least I know this won't last forever, and staying at home does give me more time to catch up with my friends," instead of thinking "Feeling this worried is AWFUL!"
  - ***High Frustration Tolerance***—This is a healthier, more rational alternative to frustration intolerance. This is when you realize that even though you may find a situation very difficult, you can stand it. For

example, you might think, "I hate feeling so anxious, but I'll just keep finding new ways to cope with it, and I'll keep going!" instead of thinking "I can't stand feeling so anxious! It's unbearable!"

- ***Anti-Self-Downing***—This is a healthier, more rational alternative to self-downing. This is when you are able to accept yourself and approve of yourself, even when you're not perfect. So for example, you might think, "Ok, I'm not handling my worries as well as I would like. I'm usually such a strong person, and now I find myself often overwhelmed. But I recognize that I'm still a good, worthwhile person, even if I'm not as strong as I thought." This thought is a more rational, positive alternative than calling yourself names like, "I'm a weak, terrible person."
- ***Anti-Other-Downing***—This is a healthier, more rational alternative to other-downing. This is when you're able to accept others, regardless of mistakes they might have made, or things they might have done to upset you. For example, you might think, "I'm pretty upset at my husband for not listening to me. But I recognize he's still generally a great guy, who does lots of great things. He picks up the kids from day care, he takes them to the doctor, and he takes care of the house." This is an alternative to thinking "He's not a good listener, and that makes him a horrible person."
- ***Anti-Life-Downing***—This is a healthier, more rational alternative to life-downing. This is when you're able to be accepting of how your life is, even when it is not exactly as you would like it to be. For example, you might think, "This isn't how I planned for my life to be, but I recognize that life is a mixed bag, full of good as well as bad events," instead of thinking "Life is meaningless and useless now that I have anxiety."

F's: New More Functional Emotions and Behaviors

- Now you're ready to see the results of all your hard work!
- By changing your negative beliefs into more helpful ones, you should now:
  - Feel better emotionally!

    For example, you may feel more positive (happier, calmer, more relaxed), or less strongly negative (e.g., anxious vs. concerned, annoyed vs. furious).
  - Behave in a more helpful way!

    For example, you may exercise, or socialize with friends, or pursue a hobby.
  - Feel better physically!

    For example, you might feel more energetic or have less muscle tension.

2.3.5 Managing Anxiety with Behavioral Techniques

Behavioral Techniques

- Sometimes when we have to deal with a stressful or challenging life situation, or when we are having a particularly hectic day, we may not have enough time or energy to focus on using the cognitive techniques we have just reviewed (i.e., A-B-C-D-E-F model) in order to manage our negative thoughts.
- On those days, the simple and brief strategies outlined below are alternative techniques you can use to help you manage any feelings of distress, negative thinking, fatigue, or other symptoms.

  (a) Activity Scheduling/Planning

    - Some people may begin to feel overwhelmed by negative thoughts when undergoing their REBT treatment as they try to fit in all their usual day-to-day activities. Planning your daily and weekly schedules in advance will help you manage your daily activities, decrease your negative thoughts, control your level of fatigue, and overall, help you feel less more in control of your life.

  (b) Distraction Techniques.

    - Distraction techniques help take your mind off of your negative thoughts. Some distraction techniques are as follows:
      - Imagining a Pleasant Image/Scene.
      - Listening to relaxing or enjoyable music tapes, CDs, videos.
      - Take a short walk.
      - Visualizing a “STOP” Sign.

2.3.6 Beyond REBT Treatment

- The REBT techniques that have been covered in this manual will help you to manage your anxiety symptoms. Moreover, these techniques can be applied to any situation in the future when you may feel overwhelmed and/or distressed.
- It is important to note that following the completion of your REBT treatment, you may occasionally experience days when you feel anxious or distressed. During such periods, we suggest that you review the contents of this manual and continue to use the REBT skills that you have learned.
- Over time and with practice, these REBT skills will become natural for you, like riding a bike or driving a car.
- We hope that you will find these techniques valuable, and we wish you every success in the future.

2.4 Recommended Readings for Patients

Drilling, E. (2002). *REBT anxiety and worry workbook* (*Rational Emotive Behavior Therapy* (*REBT*) *Learning Program*). Hazelden Information & Educational Services.

Drilling, E. (2002). *REBT anxiety and worry pamphlet* (*Rational Emotive Behavior Therapy* (*REBT*) *Learning Program*). Hazelden Information & Educational Services.

Dryden and DiGiuseppe (1990). *A primer on rational-emotive therapy*. Champaign, IL: Research Press.

Dryden, & DiGiuseppe (2007). *Ghid de terapie raţional-emotivă şi comportamentală* [A guide for rational emotive behavior therapy]. Cluj-Napoca: RTS.

On-line Resources

http://gad.about.com

References

Alford, B. A., & Beck, A. T. (1997). *The integrative power of cognitive therapy*. New York: Guilford.

American Psychiatric Association. (2000). *Diagnostic and statistical manual of mental disorders* (4th ed., text revised). Washington, DC: Author.

Beck, A. T., & Emery, G. L. (1985). *Anxiety disorders and phobias: A cognitive perspective*. New York: Basic Books.

Beck, J. S. (1995a). *Cognitive Therapy: Basics and Beyond*. New York: The Guilford Press.

Beck, A. T., & Haigh, E. A. P. (2014). Advances in cognitive theory and therapy: The generic cognitive model. *Annual Reviews of Clinical Psychology, 10*, 1–24.

Borkovec, T. D., & Costello, E. (1993). Efficacy of applied relaxation and cognitive-behavioral therapy in the treatment of generalized anxiety disorder. *Journal of Consulting and Clinical Psychology, 61*(4), 611–619.

Borkovec, T., Robinson, E., Pruzinsky, T., & DePree, J. (1983). Preliminary exploration of worry: Some characteristics and processes. *Behaviour Research and Therapy, 21*, 9–16.

Brown, T. A., Barlow, D. H., & Liebowitz, M. R. (1994). The empirical basis of generalized anxiety disorder. *The American Journal of Psychiatry, 151*(9), 1272–1280.

David, D., Kangas, M., Schnur, J. B., & Montgomery, G. H. (2004). *REBT depression manual; managing depression using rational emotive behavior therapy*. Romania: Babes-Bolyai University (BBU). (based on a general model, elaborated initially for oncological patients as a part of the American Cancer Society grant #RSGPBCPPB-108036, Dr. Guy Montgomery, principal investigator)

DiGiuseppe, R., Leaf, R., Exner, T., & Robin, M. (1988). *The development of a measure of irrational/rational thinking*. Paper presented at the meeting of the World Congress of Behavior Therapy, Edinburg, Scotland.

Dryden, W., & DiGiuseppe, R. (1990). *A primer on rational-emotive therapy*. Champaign, IL: Research Press.

Dryden, W., & Neenan, M. (2006). *Rational emotive behaviour therapy. 100 points and techniques*. Hove, England: Routledge.

Durham, R. C., Chambers, J. A., MacDonald, R. R., Power, K. G., & Major, K. (2003). Does cognitive-behavioural therapy influence the long-term outcome of generalized anxiety disorder? An 8–14 year follow-up of two clinical trials. *Psychological Medicine, 33*(3), 499–509.

Ellis, A. (1962). *Reason and emotion in psychotherapy*. New York: Lyle Stuart.
Ellis, A. (1994). *Reason and emotion in psychotherapy* (rev. ed.). Secaucus, NJ: Birch Lane.
First, M. B., Spitzer, R. L., Gibbon, M., & Williams, J. B. W. (1996). *Structured clinical interview for DSM-IV axis I disorders, clinician version (SCID-CV)*. Washington, DC: American Psychiatric Press.
Fisher, P. L., & Durham, R. C. (1999). Recovery rates in generalized anxiety disorder following psychological therapy: An analysis of clinically significant change in the STAI-T across outcome studies since 1990. *Psychological Medicine, 29*(6), 1425–1434.
Heimberg, R. G., Turk, C. L., & Mennin, D. S. (2004). *Generalized anxiety disorder. Advances in research and practice*. New York: Guilford.
Holaway, R. M., Heimberg, R. G., & Coles, M. E. (2006). A comparison of intolerance of uncertainty in analogue obsessive-compulsive disorder and generalized anxiety disorder. *Anxiety Disorders, 20*, 158–174. doi:10.1016/j.janxdis.2005.01.002.
Hollon, S. D., & Kendall, P. C. (1980). Cognitive self-statements in depression: Development of an automatic thoughts questionnaire. *Cognitive Therapy and Research, 4*(4), 383–395. doi:10.1007/BF01178214.
Kessler, R. C., & Wittchen, H. -U. (2002). Patterns and correlates of generalized anxiety disorder in community samples. *Journal of Clinical Psychiatry, 63*(suppl. 8), 4–10.
Kessler, R. C., Walters, E. E., & Wittchen, H. -U. (2004). Epidemiology. In R. G. Heimberg, C. L. Turk, & D. S. Mennin (Eds.), *Generalized anxiety disorder: Advances in research and practice* (pp. 29–50). New York: Guilford Press.
Ladouceur, R., Dugas, M. J., Freeston, M. H., Léger, E., Gagnon, F., & Thibodeau, N. (2000). Efficacy of a cognitive-behavioral treatment for generalized anxiety disorder: Evaluation in a controlled clinical trial. *Journal of Consulting and Clinical Psychology, 68*(6), 957–964.
Meyer, T. J., Miller, M. L., Metzger, R. L., & Borkovec, T. D. (1990). Development and validation of the Penn State Worry Questionnaire. *Behaviour Research and Therapy, 28*(6), 487–495.
Newman, M. G., Zuellig, A. R., Kachin, K. E., Constantino, M. J., Przeworski, A., Erickson, T., et al. (2002). Preliminary reliability and validity of the generalized anxiety disorder questionnaire-IV: A revised self-report diagnostic measure of generalized anxiety disorder. *Behavior Therapy, 33*(2), 215–233.
Ost, L. G. (1987). Applied relaxation: Description of a coping technique and review of controlled studies. *Behaviour Research and Therapy, 25*(5), 397–409.
Roemer, L., & Orsillo, S. M. (2005). An acceptance based behavior therapy for generalized anxiety disorder. In S. M. Orsillo & L. Roemer (Eds.), *Acceptance and mindfulness-based approaches to anxiety: Conceptualization and treatment* (pp. 213–240). New York: Springer.
Sibrava, N. J., & Borkovec, T. D. (2006). The cognitive avoidance theory of worry. In G. C. Davey & A. Wells (Eds.), *Worry and its psychological disorders: Theory, assessment and treatment* (pp. 239–256). Hoboken, NJ: Wiley.
Stein, M. B. (2004). Public health perspectives on generalized anxiety disorder. *Journal of Clinical Psychiatry, 65*(suppl. 13), 3–7.
Tyrer, P., & Baldwin, D. (2006). Generalized anxiety disorder. *Lancet, 368*(9553), 2156–2166.
Walen, S. R., DiGiuseppe, R., & Dryden, W. (1992). *A practitioner's guide to rational-emotive therapy* (2nd ed.). New York: Oxford University Press.
Wells, A., & King, P. (2006). Metacognitive therapy for generalized anxiety disorder: an open trial. *Journal of Behavior Therapy and Experimental Psychiatry, 37*(3), 206–212. Retrieved from http://doi.org/10.1016/j.jbtep.2005.07.002
Wittchen, H. U., & Hoyer, J. (2001). Generalized anxiety disorder: nature and course. *The Journal of Clinical Psychiatry, 62*(Suppl.11), 15–19; discussion 20–21.

Chapter 3
Rational-Emotive and Cognitive-Behavior Therapy Using Virtual Reality (RE&CBT-VR): A Short Protocol for Social Anxiety Disorder

3.1 Therapist Guide

3.1.1 Population

The RE&CBT-VR protocol is targeting adult population diagnosed with Social Anxiety Disorder according to DSM-5 (APA, 2013) as main diagnosis, the performance specifier, or public speaking subtype. This program can also be useful for people who suffer from public speaking anxiety that does not necessarily meet the diagnostic criterion of SAD, but whose occupational or educational functioning is greatly affected. This program is not indicated when (1) the SAD diagnosis is secondary to another axis I diagnosis of psychiatric disorders, like psychotic disorders, bipolar depressive disorders, current substance abuse, dementia, or mental retardation; (2) the SAD diagnosis is secondary to another axis III diagnosis; (3) personality disorders are predisposing patients to confusions between the real and virtual realities (paranoid, schizoid, schizotypal, borderline, antisocial personality disorders); or (4) the patient suffered anytime during the past 6 months of panic disorder with or without agoraphobia. Participants included in some concurrent form of psychotherapy or receiving medication are also excluded.

3.1.2 SAD and Its Treatment Using CBT/RE&CBT Interventions

According to DSM-5 (APA, 2013), social anxiety disorder is defined as "a marked fear of one or more social or performance situations in which the person is exposed to unfamiliar people or to possible scrutiny by others," like giving a speech.

I.A. Cristea et al., *REBT in the Treatment of Anxiety Disorders in Children and Adults*, SpringerBriefs in Psychology, DOI 10.1007/978-3-319-18419-7_3

The second criteria according to DSM-5 is the fear that the individual will act in a way or show anxiety symptoms that will be negatively evaluated, like being humiliated or embarrassed, which will lead to rejection. It is specified in the following two criteria that the social situations almost always provoke fear or anxiety and they are avoided or endured with intense fear or anxiety.

In order to be diagnosed as SAD, the fear or anxiety needs to be:

- Out of proportion to the actual threat posed by the social situation and to the sociocultural context.
- Persistent, typically lasting for 6 months or more.
- Causing clinically significant distress or impairment in social, occupational, or other important areas of functioning.
- Not attributable to the physiological effects of a substance or another medical condition.
- Not better explained by the symptoms of another mental disorder, such as panic disorder, body dysmorphic disorder, or autism spectrum disorder.
- Clearly unrelated or excessive, if another medical condition (e.g., Parkinson's disease, obesity, disfigurement from burns or injury) is present.

Diagnosis for treatment inclusion

Psychological assessment needs to be conducted using the SCID diagnosis (First, Spitzer, Gibbon, & Williams, 1996) for SAD and psychological testing (see Sect. 3.2).

3.1.3 The CBT/REBT's Model of SAD

It is considered (Emmelkamp et al., 2002; Rothbaum et al., 2000) that SAD is the result of processes such as classical conditioning or vicarious learning, while afterwards anxiety is maintained by the avoidance behavior of the feared social speaking situations. Cognitive processes such as irrational beliefs (Ellis & Whiteley, 1979) have been documented (Wallach, Safir, & Bar-Zvi, 2009) to play an important role in anxiety symptoms and SAD. The REBT uses the trans-diagnosis ABC model (Ellis, 1991) for conceptualizing the SAD, while other CBT approaches use specific models. Based on the REBT and the ABC model, there are two main irrational beliefs involved in SAD, namely demandingness (DEM) and awfulizing (AWF). DEM are phrased as "musts" and refer to absolutist requirements concerning own goals from self, others, and the world (e.g., I must make a good impression and I cannot conceive otherwise). Derived from DEM, when situation is against rigid goals, AWF becomes activated, and the person evaluates the particular situation as catastrophic, awful, or terrible. During RE&CBT for SAD, the irrational beliefs mentioned are approached in order to address anxiety and then conduct the exposure component using behavioral techniques.

3.1.4 CBT and VRET for SAD

In the recent years, virtual reality exposure therapy (VRET) has become a promising alternative for exposure in vivo in treating anxiety disorders, with at least same effects as the state-of-the-art treatment exposure in vivo (Powers & Emmelkamp, 2008). VRET has started to be tested, together or combined with CBT, for addressing SAD and other anxiety disorders. There are studies (Klinger et al., 2005) comparing the efficacy of VRET and CBT delivered in individual versus group formats SAD, showing that they are both similarly effective. Moreover, studies investigating the efficacy of CBT compared to combined CBT plus VRET (CBT-VRET) interventions showed (Wallach et al., 2009) that both are equally effective in the treatment of SAD. However, the study mentioned a significantly higher drop-out in the CBT group compared to the CBT-VR group (twice as many subjects). However, there are important variables documented (Price & Anderson, 2007) for modulating the effects of the CBT-VR and VR interventions, such as the presence (feeling that the environment is real) and immersion (being absorbed) during the virtual reality exposure which are moderating its impact.

Based on the evidence supporting the efficacy of CBT-VR, shorter protocols have been developed and tested for the treatment of SAD with positive results. Therefore, the four-session protocol presented below was tested in the study of Cardos, David, Lechintan, Les, & David (in preparation), currently in preparation for publication. The CBT component of this protocol is based on the mechanisms of RE&CBT, and thus is named RE&CBT-VR. This study documented a medium effect size of the RE&CBT-VR on SAD symptoms, with changes maintained at 6-month follow-up. A one session individual format of this protocol (4.5 h) was documented by Moldovan and David (2014) for a general group of patients presenting specific phobias. The sample of SAD patients included in this study was a small one (16 patients), but the effects of the intervention in their case were of high magnitude ($d=1.56$), considering the non-significant general effect found for the patients altogether.

3.2 Assessment Tools Used in RE&CBT-VR

Assessment pre-, post-intervention, and at follow-up can be done using the following self-report and other-report measures:

Diagnosis Measures

- Liebowitz Social Anxiety Scale (LSAS; Liebowitz, 1987) for assessing social anxiety severity
- Personal Report of Confidence as a Speaker (PRCS; Paul, 1966) for assessing anxiety during public speaking

- Personal Report of Communication Apprehension (PRCA-24; McCroskey et al., 1985) for assessing communication anxiety

Affective Symptom Measures

- State-Trait Anxiety Inventory (STAI; Spielberger, 1983) for assessing state and trait anxiety
- Profile of Affective Distress (PAD; Opris & Macavei, 2007) for measuring stress levels
- The Beck Depression Inventory II (BDI-II; Beck & Steer, 1987) for measuring depression severity

Behavioral Symptom Measures

- Behaviors Checklist (Stopa & Clark, 1993), for assessing participants' perception over own performance during the speech.
- Behavior Assessment Task (BAT; Beidel, Turner, Jacob, & Cooley, 1989), for a standardized assessment of patients' performance during the speech.

Physiological Measures

- Autonomic Perception Questionnaire (APQ; Mandler, Mandler, & Uviller, 1958), for assessing perception over physiological reactions during the speech.
- Autonomic arousal measured using physiological measures, like heart rate (variability), galvanic skin response, brain activity, or cortisol levels.

Cognitive Mechanisms Measures

- Self-Statements during Public Speaking (SSPS; Hofmann & DiBartolo, 2000), for assessing automatic thoughts during the speech
- Fear of Negative Evaluation (FNE; Leary, 1983; Watson & Friend, 1969), for assessing inferential cognitions specific to social anxiety
- General Attitudes and Beliefs Scale, Short Version (GABS—SV; Lindner, Kirkby, Wertheim, & Birch, 2007)
- Public Speaking Rational and Irrational Beliefs Scale (PS-RIBS; David, unpublished; see Appendix)

Virtual Reality Presence and Immersion Measures

- Presence Questionnaire (PQ; Witmer, & Singer, 1998) for assessing presence during virtual reality exposure.
- The Immersion Questionnaire (ImQ; Zimand, Anderson, Gershon, Graap, Hodges, & Rothbaum, 2001) for assessing how real the virtual reality exposure was for patients.

3.3 Rational-Emotive and Cognitive-Behavior Therapy Using Virtual Reality (RE&CBT-VR) for Social Anxiety Disorder (SAD): A Short Protocol in Four Sessions

The RECBT-VR intervention consists of four modules, among which two are group sessions and two individual sessions. The first and last sessions are delivered in group format, while the exposure sessions are delivered individually.

3.3.1 Key Elements of the RE&CBT-VR Intervention

The basic characteristics of the RE&CBT-VR intervention for SAD:

1. The cognitive–behavioral conceptualization of the problem, based on the ABCDE model and specific model of SAD.
2. Focusing on changing specific irrational beliefs relevant for public speaking.
3. The use of cognitive, biological, and behavioral techniques for changing the irrational beliefs into rational beliefs.
4. The use of rational coping statements in the form of "psychological pills" (David, 2006).
5. The use of biological techniques (e.g., gradual exposure) for addressing social anxiety symptoms.
6. The use of homework.

The therapist delivering the RE&CBT-VR protocol uses a wide variety of techniques with the aim to replace irrational thinking patterns during public speaking with rational ones.

The cognitive techniques used in the intervention consist of identifying own irrational beliefs and replacing them with rational ones. A particular attention is given to DEM and AWF types of irrational beliefs. Personalized coping cards in the form of "psychological pills" are developed by the patients during treatment.

The biological techniques employed are relaxation techniques like controlled breathing. The patient is practicing such abilities for being able to control excessive physiological arousal and prevent potential panic attack situations during exposure.

The behavioral techniques used are concerning breaking up the avoidance vicious circle, by gradual exposure to the feared stimuli. The patient is developing a personalized list of the stimuli relative to their gradual levels of anxiety severity. They are exposed in virtual reality environments and then in vivo.

The virtual reality environment consists of a computer, 3D head-mounted-display (HMD), and headphones. The computer supporting the VR HMD system has the following characteristics: Intel® Core™ 2 Duo Processor T7600, 1 GB RAM, NVIDIA, GeForce 7900 eMagin Z800 HMD (inertial head tracking), and headphones. The public speaking soft was developed by Virtually Better, Inc.

3.3.2 Session Structure

The short RE&CBT-VR intervention consists of two 90-min group therapy sessions and two individual 30 min exposure sessions. Group sessions should include between 6 and 8 patients. Both group and individual sessions are highly structured.

The sessions has the following general format (Beck, 1995):

- Brief update and mood check
- Bridge from previous session
- Setting the agenda
- Review homework
- Addressing the agenda
- Summary
- Assign homework
- Feedback

The first group session has the following structure:

- Bridge from previous session (assessment)
- Setting the agenda
- Psycho-education about therapy, VR, and SAD
- Normalizing expectancies
- SAD conceptualization using the ABC model
- Generating own "psychological pills"
- Training in controlled breathing as relaxation strategy
- Completing own Subjective Units of Distress (SUDS) for gradual exposure
- Summary
- Homework assignment (to prepare a speech)
- Feedback

The second individual VR exposure sessions has the following structure:

- Bridge from previous session
- Setting the agenda
- Psycho-education about the VR devices
- Provision of safety norms and risks information
- Gradual exposure based on SUDS in the virtual classroom environment
- Using the "Psychological pills" and controlled breathing for managing anxiety during exposure
- Debriefing
- Homework assignment (to prepare a speech)
- Feedback

The third individual VR exposure sessions has the following structure:

- Bridge from previous session
- Setting the agenda
- Psycho-education about the VR devices
- Provision of safety norms and risks information
- Gradual exposure based on SUDS in the virtual auditorium environment
- Using the "Psychological pills" and controlled breathing for managing anxiety during exposure
- Debriefing
- Homework assignment (to prepare a speech)
- Feedback

The final (fourth) group session has the following structure:

- Bridge from previous session
- Setting the agenda
- In vivo exposure (giving a 5 min speech in front of the group)
- Debriefing and gain consolidation
- Summary
- Homework assignment (to plan another ecologic exposure)
- Feedback

Appendix: Forms and Handouts for the RE&CBT-VR

The ABC monitoring form (David et al., 2014; Ellis, 1956, 1991—reproduced with permission)

A ACTIVATING EVENT	C CONSEQUENCES
	Unhealthy Negative Emotions Maladaptive Behaviors:
• Shortly present the distressing situation (A) (e.g., what would record a video camera?)	Some of the unhealthy negative emotions can be: • Fear-Anxiety • Anger • Jealousy • Depression • Shame • Guilt, etc.

B's Negative or Unhelpful Beliefs	D's Disputing / Restructuring the Unhelpful Beliefs	E's Effective/Helpful Beliefs	F's Functional Emotions and Behaviors
			New healthier emotions: **New more adaptive behaviors:**

Subjective Units of Distress (SUDS; Wolpe, 1969)

The subjective units of distress scale specify 11 points on the scale, ranging from 0 (absolutely complete relaxation) up to 10 (extreme distress).

Anxiety level	Description	Situation
Zero	Complete relaxation. Deep sleep, no distress at all	
One	Awake but very relaxed; dosing off. Your mind wanders and drifts, similar to what you might feel just prior to falling asleep	
Two	Relaxing at the beach, relaxing at home in front of a warm fire on a wintry day, or walking peacefully in the woods	
Three	The amount of tension and stress needed to keep your attention from wandering, to keep your head erect, and so on. This tension and stress is not experienced as unpleasant; it is "normal"	
Four	Mild distress such as mild feelings of bodily tension, mild worry, mild apprehension, mild fear, or mild anxiety. Somewhat unpleasant but easily tolerated	
Five	Mild to moderate distress. Distinctly unpleasant but insufficient to produce many bodily symptoms	
Six	Moderate distress. Very unpleasant feelings of fear, anxiety, anger, worry, apprehension, and/or substantial bodily tension such as a headache or upset stomach. Distinctly unpleasant but tolerable sensations; you're still able to think clearly. What most people would describe as a "bad day," but your ability to work, drive, converse, and so on is not impeded	
Seven	Moderately high distress that makes concentration hard. Fairly intense bodily distress	
Eight	High distress. High levels of fear, anxiety, worry, apprehension, and/or bodily tension. These feelings cannot be tolerated very long. Thinking and problem-solving is impaired. Bodily distress is substantial. Ability to work, drive, converse, and so on is difficult	
Nine	High to extreme distress. Thinking is substantially impaired	
Ten	Extreme distress, panic- and/or terror-stricken, extreme bodily tension. The maximum amount of fear, anxiety, and/or apprehension you can possibly imagine	

"Psychological Pills" for Public Speaking

Based on the PsyPills app (Gavita, 2013)

I want very much to make a good presentation, but I realize that things do not necessarily have to be as I wish.

I want very much to make a good impression and not embarrass myself during my presentation, but I realize that things do not necessarily have to be as I wish.

I want very much to perfectly master the topic, speak fluently, and find the adequate answers during the presentation, but I realize that it does not necessarily have to be as I wish.

I want very much not to feel anxious, blush, or have trembling voice during the presentation, but I do realize that it does not necessarily have to be as I wish.

It would be very uncomfortable if I would make a weak presentation and I am making all the efforts not to happen, but this would not be awful.

It would be very uncomfortable if, despite my efforts, I would not be appreciated by the audience or I would embarrass myself during the presentation, but it would not be awful.

It would be very uncomfortable not to find my words during the presentation and/or the audience to realize that I do not perfectly master the topic, but not the worst thing.

It would be very unpleasant to feel anxious, blush, or have trembling voice during the presentation, but it would not be awful.

In case I cannot answer properly questions from the audience, I can accept the people in the audience as human beings.

In case people in the audience are not approving or are criticizing/despising me, I think this does not impact their worth.

In case someone asks me difficult questions and I get blocked, I understand this does not impact their worth.

In case I am feeling very anxious, blush, or have trembling voice during the presentation, I understand this does not impact the worth of my audience.

In case I am making a weak presentation, I can accept myself having the same value as a human being and to improve my behavior.
In case I am making a bad impression or the public is uninterested on my presentation, I can accept myself having the same value and to improve my behavior.
In case I *do not perfectly* master the topic, find my words, or not know the answers to the questions coming from the public, I understand that this does not impact my worth as a person.
In case I feel very anxious, blush, or have trembling voice during the presentation, I understand that this does not impact my worth as a person.

It would be very unpleasant to make a weak and flawed presentation, but I could stand it in case it would happen.
It would be very unpleasant if the audience would make a bad impression of me during the presentation, but I could stand it in case it would happen.
It would be very uncomfortable to get blocked/not find my words during the presentation or to not be able to answer to the questions from the public, but I could tolerate it in case it happens.
It would be very uncomfortable to feel anxious, blush, or have trembling voice during the presentation, but I could tolerate it in case it happens.

In case someone asks me difficult questions and I get blocked, I understand this does not impact their worth.
In case I make a bad presentation, I can accept life with its ups and downs and I can keep improving my skills.
In case people in the audience are not approving or are criticizing/ despising me, I can accept life with its ups and downs and I can keep improving my skills.

In case I *do not perfectly* master the topic, find my words, or not know the answers to the questions, I can accept life with its ups and downs and I can keep improving my skills
In case I feel very anxious, blush, or have trembling voice during the presentation, I can accept life with its ups and downs and I can keep improving my skills

Measures

Public Speaking: Rational and Irrational Beliefs Scale

Name: Today's Date: _/_/_ Age: ___ Sex: Male or Female

When making a presentation or a public speech in front of an audience, some people tend to think that situation absolutely must be the way they want (in terms of absolute must). In the same situation, other people think in preferential terms and accept the situation, even if they want very much that those situations do not happen. In light of these possibilities, please estimate how much the statements below represent the thoughts that you have when by yourself in public places.

Please think about a situation when you ***were*** *making* ***a presentation or a public speech in front of an audience or preparing one****. Try and recall the thoughts that you have had in such situations.*

Using the following scale, indicate in the space provided *how true each of these statements is for you.*

1. Strongly agree
2. Somewhat agree
3. Somewhat disagree
4. Strongly disagree

3.3.2.1 Part 1—Performance RIBS

		Strongly agree	Somewhat agree	Somewhat disagree	Strongly disagree
1	I absolutely must make a good presentation, and I cannot conceive otherwise	1	2	3	4
2	I want very much to make a good presentation, but I realize that things do not necessarily have to be as I wish	1	2	3	4
3	It would be awful and terrifying if, despite my efforts, I would make a weak presentation	1	2	3	4
4	It would be very uncomfortable if I would make a weak presentation and I am making all the efforts not to happen, but it would not be awful	1	2	3	4
5	If I am making a weak presentation, this shows that I am worthless and a loser	1	2	3	4

(continued)

(continued)

		Strongly agree	Somewhat agree	Somewhat disagree	Strongly disagree
6	If I am making a weak presentation, I can accept myself having the same value as a human being and to improve my behavior	1	2	3	4
7	If I cannot answer properly questions from the audience, this is because people in the audience are bad and worthless beings	1	2	3	4
8	If I cannot answer properly questions from the audience, I can accept the people in the audience as human beings	1	2	3	4
9	I could not stand to make a weak and flawed presentation	1	2	3	4
10	It would be extremely unpleasant to make a weak and flawed presentation, but I could stand it in case it would happen	1	2	3	4
11	If I make a bad presentation, it means life is unfair and not worth the effort	1	2	3	4
12	If I make a bad presentation, I can accept life with its ups and downs and I can keep improving my skills	1	2	3	4

3.3.2.2 Part 2—Approval RIBS

		Strongly agree	Somewhat agree	Somewhat disagree	Strongly disagree
1	I absolutely must make a good impression and not embarrass myself during my presentation, and I cannot conceive otherwise	1	2	3	4
2	I want very much to make a good impression and not embarrass myself during my presentation, but I realize that things do not necessarily have to be as I wish	1	2	3	4
3	It would be awful and terrifying if, despite my efforts, I would not make a good impression or embarrass myself during the presentation	1	2	3	4

(continued)

(continued)

		Strongly agree	Somewhat agree	Somewhat disagree	Strongly disagree
4	It would be very uncomfortable if, despite my efforts, I would be not appreciated by the audience or I would embarrass myself during the presentation, but it would not be awful	1	2	3	4
5	If I am making a bad impression or the public is uninterested on my presentation, this shows that I am worthless and a loser	1	2	3	4
6	If I am making a bad impression or the public is uninterested on my presentation, I can accept myself having the same value and to improve my behavior	1	2	3	4
7	If people in the audience are not approving or are criticizing/despising me, this shows what bad and worthless beings they are	1	2	3	4
8	If people in the audience are not approving or are criticizing/despising me, I think this does not impact their worth	1	2	3	4
9	I could not stand if the audience would make a bad impression on me during the presentation	1	2	3	4
10	It would be very unpleasant if the audience would make a bad impression of me during the presentation, but I could stand it in case it would happen	1	2	3	4
11	If people in the audience are not approving or are criticizing/despising me, it means life is unfair and not worth the effort	1	2	3	4
12	If people in the audience are not approving or are criticizing/despising me, I can accept life with its ups and downs and I can keep improving my skills	1	2	3	4

3.3.2.3 Part 3—Communication RIBS

		Strongly agree	Somewhat agree	Somewhat disagree	Strongly disagree
1	I must perfectly master the topic, speak fluently, and find the adequate answers during the presentation and I cannot conceive otherwise	1	2	3	4
2	I want very much to perfectly master the topic, speak fluently, and find the adequate answers during the presentation, but I realize that it does not necessarily have to be as I wish	1	2	3	4
3	I could not stand to get blocked/not find my words during the presentation or to not be able to answer all the questions from the public	1	2	3	4
4	It would be very uncomfortable to get blocked/not find my words during the presentation or to not be able to answer the questions from the public, but I could tolerate it in case it happens	1	2	3	4
5	If someone asks me difficult questions and I get blocked, this shows it is a bad and worthless person	1	2	3	4
6	If someone asks me difficult questions and I get blocked, I understand this does not impact their worth	1	2	3	4
7	It would be awful not to find my words during the presentation and the audience to realize that I do not perfectly master the topic I am talking about	1	2	3	4
8	It would be very uncomfortable not to find my words during the presentation and the audience to realize that I do not perfectly master the topic, but not the worst thing	1	2	3	4
9	If I *do not perfectly* master the topic, find my words or not know the answers to the questions coming from the public, this shows I am an incompetent and a worthless person	1	2	3	4

		Strongly agree	Somewhat agree	Somewhat disagree	Strongly disagree
10	If I *do not perfectly* master the topic, find my words or not know the answers to the questions coming from the public, I understand that this does not impact my worth as a person	1	2	3	4
11	If I *do not perfectly* master the topic, find my words or not know the answers to the questions, this shows life is unfair and not worth the effort	1	2	3	4
12	If I *do not perfectly* master the topic, find my words or not know the answers to the questions, I can accept life with its ups and downs and I can keep improving my skills	1	2	3	4

3.3.2.4 Part 4—Comfort RIBS

		Strongly agree	Somewhat agree	Somewhat disagree	Strongly disagree
1	I absolutely must not feel anxious, blush, or have trembling voice during the presentation and I cannot conceive otherwise	1	2	3	4
2	I want very much not to feel very anxious, blush, or have trembling voice during the presentation, but I do realize that it does not necessarily have to be as I wish	1	2	3	4
3	I could not stand to feel anxious, blush, or have trembling voice during the presentation	1	2	3	4
4	It would be very uncomfortable to feel anxious, blush, or have trembling voice during the presentation, but I could tolerate it in case it happens	1	2	3	4
5	If I am feeling very anxious, blush, or have trembling voice during the presentation, this shows others are bad and worthless people	1	2	3	4
6	If I am feeling very anxious, blush, or have trembling voice during the presentation, I understand this does not impact others' worth	1	2	3	4

(continued)

(continued)

		Strongly agree	Somewhat agree	Somewhat disagree	Strongly disagree
7	It would be awful to feel very anxious, blush, or have trembling voice during the presentation	1	2	3	4
8	It would be very unpleasant to feel anxious, blush, or have trembling voice during the presentation, but it would not be awful	1	2	3	4
9	If I feel very anxious, blush, or have trembling voice during the presentation, this shows I am a weak and a worthless person	1	2	3	4
10	If I feel very anxious, blush, or have trembling voice during the presentation, I understand that this does not impact my worth as a person	1	2	3	4
11	If I feel very anxious, blush, or have trembling voice during the presentation, this shows life is unfair and not worth the effort				
12	If I feel very anxious, blush, or have trembling voice during the presentation, I can accept life with its ups and downs and I can keep improving my skills				

References

American Psychiatric Association. (2013). *Diagnostic and statistical manual of mental disorders* (5th ed.). Washington, DC: Author.

Beck, J. S. (1995). *Cognitive Therapy: Basics and Beyond.* New York: The Guilford Press.

Beck, A. T., & Steer, R. A. (1987). *Beck depression inventory—Manual.* San Antonio, TX: The Psychological Association.

Beidel, D. C., Turner, S. M., Jacob, R. G., & Cooley, M. R. (1989). Assessment of social phobia: Reliability of an impromptu speech task. *Journal of Anxiety Disorders, 3*, 149–158.

Cardoş, R. A. I., David, O. A., Lechinţan, I., Leş, A., David, D. O. Is VRCBT more effective than VRET? Efficacy of virtual reality based cognitive-behavioral therapy versus virtual reality exposure therapy in social anxiety disorder: Superiority randomized clinical trial, Posttreatment outcomes, and six-month follow-up. Manuscript in preparation.

David, D. (2006). *Rational treatments: Evidence-based psychological treatments for major depressive disorder.* Bucuresti, Romania: Tritonic.

David, O. A., Matu, A., Pintea, S., Cotet, C., & Nagy, D. (2014). Cognitive-behavioral processes based on using the ABC analysis by trainees' for their personal development. *Journal of Rational-Emotive and Cognitive-Behavioral Therapy, 32*(3), 198–215.

Ellis, A. (1956). *The ABC model of rational emotive therapy.* Paper presented at the American Psychological Association (APA) Convention, Chicago, IL.

Ellis, A. (1991). The revised ABC's of rational-emotive therapy (RET). *Journal of Rational-Emotive & Cognitive-Behavior Therapy, 9*(3), 139–172.

Ellis, A., & Whiteley, J. M. (1979). *Theoretical and empirical foundations of rational-emotive therapy*. Pacific Grove, CA: Thomson Brooks/Cole.

Emmelkamp, P. G. M., Krijn, M., Hulsbosch, A. M., de Vries, S., Schuemie, M. J., & van der Mast, C. A. P. G. (2002). Virtual reality treatment versus exposure in vivo: A comparative evaluation in acrophobia. *Behaviour Research & Therapy, 40*(5), 509–516.

First, M. B., Spitzer, R. L., Gibbon, M., & Williams, J. B. W. (1996). *Structured clinical interview for DSM-IV axis I disorders, clinician version (SCID-CV)*. Washington, DC: American Psychiatric Press.

Gavita, O. A. (2013). PsyPills (Version 3.0) [Mobile application software]. Retrieved from https://itunes.apple.com/us/app/psypills/id589004229?mt=8.

Klinger, E., Bouchard, S., Légeron, P., Roy, S., Lauer, F., Chemin, I., et al. (2005). Virtual reality therapy versus cognitive behavior therapy for social phobia: A preliminary controlled study. *Cyberpsychology & Behavior, 8*, 76–88.

Hofmann, S. G., & DiBartolo, P. M. (2000). An instrument to assess self-statements during public speaking: Scale development and preliminary psychometric properties. *Behavior Therapy, 31*, 499–515.

Leary, M. R. (1983). Social anxiousness: The construct and its measurement. *Journal of Personality Assessment, 47*, 66–75.

Liebowitz, M. R. (1987). Social phobia. *Modern Problems of Pharmacopsychiatry, 22*, 141–173.

Lindner, H., Kirkby, R., Wertheim, E., & Birch, P. (1999). A brief assessment of irrational thinking: The Shortened General Attitude and Belief Scale. *Cognitive Therapy and Research, 23*, 651–663.

Mandler, G., Mandler, J. M., & Uviller, E. T. (1958). Autonomic feedback: The perception of autonomic activity. *Journal of Abnormal and Social Psychology, 56*, 367–373.

McCroskey, J. C., Beatty, M. J., Kearney, P., & Plax, T. G. (1985). The content validity of the PRCA-24 as a measure of communication apprehension across communication contexts. *Communication Quarterly, 33*(3), 165–173.

Moldovan, R., & David, D. (2014). One session treatment of cognitive and behavioral therapy and virtual reality for social and specific phobias. Preliminary results from a randomized clinical trial. *Journal of Cognitive and Behavioral Psychotherapies, 14*(1), 67–83.

Opris, D., & Macavei, B. (2007). The profile of emotional distress: Norms for the Romanian population. *Journal of Cognitive & Behavioral Psychotherapies, 7*(2), 139–158.

Paul, G. L. (1966). *Insight vs. desensitization in psychotherapy: An experiment in anxiety reduction*. Stanford, CA: Stanford University Press.

Powers, M. B., & Emmelkamp, P. M. G. (2008). Virtual reality exposure therapy for anxiety disorders: A meta-analysis. *Journal of Anxiety Disorders, 22*, 561–569.

Price, M., & Anderson, P. (2007). The role of presence in virtual reality exposure therapy. *Journal of Anxiety Disorders*, 21(5),742–751.doi:10.1016/j.janxdis.2006.11.002

Spielberger, C. D. (1983). *Manual for the State—Trait Anxiety Inventory (Form Y)*. Palo Alto, CA: Mind Garden.

Stopa, L., & Clark, D. M. (1993). Cognitive processes in social phobia. *Behaviour Research Therapy, 31*, 255–267.

Watson, D., & Friend, R. (1969). Measurement of social-evaluative anxiety. *Journal of Consulting and Clinical Psychology, 33*, 448–457.

Wallach, H. S., Safir, M. P., & Bar-Zvi, M. (2009). Virtual reality cognitive behavior therapy for public speaking anxiety; a randomized clinical trial. *Behavior Modification, 33*(3), 314–338.

Witmer, B. G., & Singer, M. J. (1998). Measuring presence in virtual environments: A presence questionnaire. *Presence: Teleoperators and Virtual Environments, 7*(3), 225–240.

Wolpe, J. (1969). *The practice of behavior therapy*. New York: Pergamon Press.

Zimand, E., Anderson, P., Gershon, J., Graap, K., Hodges, L., & Rothbaum, B. O. (2001). Virtual reality therapy: Innovative treatment of anxiety disorders. *Primary Psychiatry, 9*, 51–54.

Further Reading

DiGiuseppe, R. A., Doyle, K. A., Dryden, W., & Backx, W. (2014). *A practitioner's guide to rational-emotive behavior therapy* (3rd ed.). New York: Oxford University Press.

Dryden, W., DiGiuseppe, R., & Neenan, M. (2010). *A primer on rational emotive behavioral therapy* (3rd ed.). Champaign, IL: Research Press.

Ellis, A., & Harper, R. (1961). *A new guide to rational living*. Englewood Cliffs, NJ: Prentice-Hall.

Part II
Treatment of Anxiety Disorders in Children and Adolescents

Chapter 4
Rational-Emotive and Cognitive-Behavior Therapy (RE&BT) Treatment Protocol for Anxiety in Children and Adolescents

4.1 The Causes of Childhood Anxiety Disorders

Anxiety is transmitted from parents to children both genetically and environmentally (Creswell, Murray, Stacey, & Cooper, 2011). On the one hand, biologic vulnerability to anxiety explains up to 30–40 % of anxiety variability, while environmental factors account for the rest (Barlow, 2002). On the other hand, the way parents conduct exposure to the environment, the way they react to new, uncertain, or ambiguous stimuli, and the reinforcements and punishments they apply, all can model anxious emotional responses and behaviors. While inborn personality features such as neuroticism favor anxious responses, fear is learned in the environment, and there are several mechanisms which can explain how a child learns to be afraid of particular stimuli and situations:

1. *Classical conditioning*—direct exposure to feared situations. The idea that anxiety disorders can be understood as emotional conditioned responses was supported by James Watson, who conducted a conditioning experiment with a little child, known as "little Albert." Albert was made to fear rats because the experimenters associated the presence of the rat (conditional stimulus) with a powerful noise which the child had feared before (unconditioned stimulus). Exposure to traumatic situations (e.g., being bitten by a dog, being in an accident) can thus lead to anxiety through classical conditioning (Watson & Rayner, 1920).
2. *Operant/instrumental conditioning* explains learning new behaviors due to both antecedents (what happens before conducting the behavior) and consequences (what follows behaviors—reinforcements or punishments), as described by Skinner (1974). With relevance to anxiety disorders, if a child, for example, wants to join other children playing and he is constantly cast away, this may lead to social anxiety. Or, if the parents overly valor carefulness and punish exploratory behaviors, this may lead to anxiety as well.
3. *Vicarious learning*—in this direction, Bandura (1977) advanced the idea that anxiety can be learned by example, by vicarious learning. From very young ages,

I.A. Cristea et al., *REBT in the Treatment of Anxiety Disorders in Children and Adults*, SpringerBriefs in Psychology, DOI 10.1007/978-3-319-18419-7_4

children are attentive to other's reactions and often imitate them. When dealing with a novel situation, a child would often look around to see how the others (especially the significant persons) react. While the process is adaptive in itself, preventing the child from suffering when real dangers are present, it has the disadvantage that it can model overly anxious behavior. For example, if a parent has an exaggerated fear reaction when the child falls, the child learns to fear such situations and limits her range of activities.

However, even when exposed to the same behavioral mechanisms, as those described above, some children develop anxiety and others do not. While, as mentioned before, genetics plays an important part, the way children interpret what is happening (i.e., cognitions) ultimately makes the difference. Anxiety is characterized by distorted thinking, some of the features of anxious thinking being outlined by Clark and Beck (2010):

1. A distorted perception of danger—anxious individuals overestimate the danger associated with certain stimuli, or the likelihood of them occurring.
2. Helplessness—the belief one is not able to deal with the anxiety-arousing stimuli.
3. Diminishing the perception of positive stimuli.
4. Difficulties in using reflexive thinking—this would aid a realistic assessment of danger.
5. Distorted automatic processes are faster than elaborate ones—thus, conditioned fear responses take place much faster than rational thinking; so we can still fear something although we know rationally that it can't hurt us.
6. The vicious circle of anxiety, where the individuals interpret her anxiety symptoms in a catastrophic way, thus leading to increasing anxiety (i.e., fear of fear).
7. The activation of threat schemas and perceiving oneself as weak, helpless, and vulnerable in dealing with the feared situation.

4.2 The Treatment of Childhood Anxiety Disorders

Given the high prevalence, early onset, persistence, and chronic nature of childhood anxiety disorders, the need for early specialized interventions is much warranted. Since the efficiency of medication in childhood anxiety disorders has not been clearly established (see, for example, Wagner et al., 2003), and many parents refuse to administer medication to their children due to potential side-effects, psychological treatments represent the first line of intervention for anxious youth (see National Institute for Health and Clinical Excellence guidelines—www.guidance.nice.org.uk; see also Marshall & Ramchandani, 2008).

Cognitive–behavioral therapy has been shown to be an efficacious treatment of anxiety disorders in children, with average remission rates ranging from 56 to 67 % at post-treatment (Cartwright-Hatton, Roberts, Chitsabesan, Fothergill, & Harrington, 2004; James, Soler, & Weatherall, 2005; Silverman, Pina, & Viswesvaran, 2008). CBT protocols include as main components (1) guiding the child through graded exposure (in vivo or imaginary), and (2) assisting the child in developing coping skills and cognitive self-control strategies (Silverman & Motoca, 2011). CBT also includes parents in treatment, their involvement being expected to enhance the therapeutic effects. However, even if cognitive behavioral therapy has serious scientific support and proven efficiency in the treatment of anxiety disorders for children and adolescents, long-term improvements in anxiety symptoms are still inconclusively documented (James, James, Cowdrey, Soler, & Choke, 2013). Therefore, developing new, more effective, and more accessible interventions for childhood anxiety is highly warranted. In this chapter, we will further present an REBT-based protocol for childhood anxiety implemented through a computerized platform.

As the main principles of REBT have been presented in the previous chapters, we will focus on its particularities when applied with children. Similarly to adults, children often make distorted inferences (arbitrary inferences, overgeneralizations, selective abstracting, minimizing, maximizing; Beck, 1976) and subsequently, distorted evaluations (demandingness, awfulizing, low frustration tolerance, global evaluation; Ellis, 1994), which further lead to dysfunctional emotions, including anxiety. Specifically with reference to anxiety, Ellis (1982) distinguished between *ego anxiety*—anxiety in relation to the self in terms of value and lovability (believing that one must do well and be approved by others, and if he/she is not, then the self becomes worthless and unlovable), and *discomfort anxiety*—fearing that awful things will happen and one will get hurt. In this framework, social and performance anxiety would be forms of ego anxiety, while specific phobias and generalized anxiety would be labeled as discomfort anxiety.

When working with children, REBT therapists take into account developmental particularities and adjust flexibly their techniques in order to address emotional disturbances in children in an age-appropriate manner (Bernard & Joyce, 1984). For example, little disputing is attempted with children younger than six and more sophisticated forms of disputing (i.e., logical) are only introduced with children older than 11–12. It is not that rational thinking is not promoted with children, but therapists do that in an age-adapted manner. With young children for example, therapists can introduce rational self-talk (e.g., "even if it difficult, I can do it; even if I dislike it, I can stand it") directly, without disputing irrational beliefs first, especially because young children have little capacity for abstract reasoning. Also, before reaching the formal operations stage, at about 12, children are taught the principles or REBT using specific, concrete examples from the child's life, and not hypothetical scenarios, and therapists often rely in their presentations on visual, graphic materials or stories (DiGiuseppe & Bernard, 2006). Last but not the least, REBT with children aims for including relevant others in the intervention, such as peers, parents, or teachers (Woulff, 1983).

4.3 REBT for Childhood Anxiety Disorders: A Treatment Protocol

We will next present the treatment protocol which is currently tested with children with various anxiety disorders, within an undergoing project implemented in Romania. The protocol includes a therapist guide and therapeutic resources adapted for working with children. Children aged 10–16 years with various anxiety disorders according to the DSM-5 are included in the study.

4.4 REBT for Childhood Anxiety Disorders: Therapist Guide

*Note: This session by session treatment protocol is based on REBT manuals (Ellis & Bernard, 2006), REBT treatment protocols for other emotional disorders in children (*e.g., *depression; Iftene et al., 2014), and on empirically validated CBT protocols for childhood anxiety disorders (*i.e., *Kendall,* 1994; *Kendall & Southam-Gerow,* 1996; *Shortt, Barrett, & Fox,* 2001*).*

4.4.1 Key Elements of the REBT Intervention

The key elements of this treatment protocol consist in teaching the child/adolescents the distinction between functional and dysfunctional emotions, respectively rational and irrational beliefs. Unlike other cognitive–behavioral treatment protocols (e.g., Kendall, 1994), the child is not taught anxiety is a normal reaction, but rather that fear is normal/functional, while anxiety is abnormal/dysfunctional. In addition, the protocol is designed to allow sufficient flexibility in such a way that it can be used for a wider age range compared with other CBT protocols for anxiety and can accommodate the entire range of anxiety symptoms (including panic attacks and specific phobias).

4.4.2 Session Structure

The REBT intervention for anxiety disorders in children consists of 14 weekly, individual 50-min sessions, plus two parent sessions. All the sessions are highly structured: for every of the sessions the therapist has an agenda (updated at the start of the session), which lists aspects that will be dealt with during the session. In principle, the therapist has a general structure of the agenda for every session (according to the flow of the treatment protocol): the agenda will always include a review of the previous week's homework, and one or two of the specific issues which will be the main focus of the session. However, the contents of the agenda will be personalized according to the specific needs of every treated child. In addition, the child (or parent, in the case of parent session) and therapist will always agree on the contents of the agenda at the beginning of the session.

Every session will start with a brief update and mood check, followed by bridging the connection with the previous session. Then, the therapist and patient (or parent, when applicable) set the agenda for the current session. Next, the homework will be reviewed, then the items on the agenda will be discussed. Before assigning a new homework, the therapist will assist the patient in summarizing the session. Finally, the therapist will ask for the patient's feedback for the current session.

***The initial phase of the treatment* (*weeks 1–7*)** will include the first two sessions addressed to child/adolescent, and the first session addressed to parent/legal guardian. We detail below the structure recommended for every session of the initial phase of the treatment:

4.4.2.1 Sessions 1–2

These are introductory sessions, dedicated to the child/adolescent. They will be designed to include the following aspects:

Clinical diagnosis and assessment. Prior to be enrolled in the psychotherapeutic process, the children should have undergone a complete psychological assessment process. This protocol is aimed to be used with youth having a principal diagnosis of anxiety or whose anxiety symptoms are the principal elements of the clinical presentation. During the first session, therapist should pay special attention to any changes that might occur since psychological assessment. The present emotional status of the child should be evaluated also by means of standardized scales, like the *Spence Children Anxiety Scale* (Spence, 1998) or *Multidimensional Anxiety Scale for Children* (MASC; March et al., 1997)—and the child should be informed about the utility of doing so.

Starting to build the therapeutic relationship. This is maybe the cornerstone aspect of the first session—that is why the therapist should allocate specific resources for this. It is essential to make the child/adolescent feel comfortable and secure within the session. In order to do so, therapist may start the discussion with a topic that presents interest for the patient[1]—and stimulate the child/adolescent to speak about himself. Also, it is important to discuss the issue of confidentiality—therapist should explain to the child/adolescent that (s)he is the patient, nor her/his parents/legal guardians, and the therapist will not discuss with those any aspects of the therapy without the consent of the child. However, the limits of the confidentiality should be set firmly: if anything put at the risk the patient and/or others, the therapist will divulgate any information that can prevent the danger. If stimulating the child/adolescent to speak about himself proves difficult, therapist can make use of a story or clinical vignette to discuss with the young patient the problems, reactions, and motives of a virtual character. When applicable, therapist may want to reserve around 10 min at the end of the session to do a relaxing activity with the patient—like playing a game or watching a funny, short video.

Teaching child about positive/negative and functional/dysfunctional emotions, with a special emphasis on anxiety (i.e., help him/her understand how anxiety is a dysfunctional emotion and what would be its functional counterpart). The distinction between functional and dysfunctional emotions represents one of the marks of the REBT. The child should understand that the goal of the therapy will not be the

[1] Based on the information obtained during the assessment phase.

elimination of the negative emotions—but rather using them adaptively. Apparently, this would be difficult for a child to understand—but the therapist can use analogies, vignettes, and case examples to illustrate the differences between functional and dysfunctional emotions, and to help child understand negative emotions are normal and *necessary* parts of the life. The difference between fear and anxiety should be stated clearly, based on cognitive and behavioral hallmarks (see Sect. 4.5 for details).

Promoting the young patient's understanding of his/her own anxiety disorder(s). Therapist should aim at helping the child understand how his/her anxiety looks like (i.e., which are the emotional, psychophysiological, cognitive, and behavioral components of his/her anxiety), in order to be able to adequately identify anxiety when it occurs. To that end, checklists of anxious symptoms can be used. Then, therapist and patient will build a hierarchy of the anxiety-linked situations (which will be latter used for devising in-session exercises and prescribing homework).

Encouraging child to understand the linkage between his/her anxiety and other emotional problems (secondary emotions). Most of the anxious youths presents multiple anxiety problems (e.g., social anxiety, generalized anxiety disorder, panic attacks, etc.) and/or develop second order emotional problems (e.g., depression or anxiety about anxiety), due to their inability to adequately manage the original anxiety problem. The second order emotional problems interfere often with the therapeutic process targeting the primary emotional problem (i.e., anxiety). Thus, therapist will help the child understand how emotions co-occur frequently, or are "chained," and why "unchaining" them would smooth the therapeutic process. Again, case examples or vignettes could be useful means of illustrating the linkage between anxiety and other emotional problems, prior to discuss this topic at a personal level with the young participant.

Education for psychotherapy and REBT, and adjusting treatments expectations. Therapist should make as clear as possible for the patient what is psychotherapy, how the therapeutic process will unfold, what will be the specific aspects targeted in psychotherapy, how and when the gains will be evident. The importance of completing the homework assignments and taking personal responsibility for change will be emphasized.

Promoting the commitment for the therapy. To do this, the therapist can ask the child/adolescent to imagine how her/his life would look like if no problems of anxiety were present (e.g., what s/he do differently, what new experiences s/he could enjoy, etc.). Based on this imaginary exercise, the therapist and the patient can agree on goals of the therapy.

Homework Suggestions for the First Two Sessions

- Identifying different emotions in others
- Self-monitoring of emotional reactions and observing how they interfere with or promote adaptation (with an emphasis on anxiety; see the ABC model in Sect. 4.5)
- Noting how the child reacts when anxious (i.e., self-monitoring of anxious symptoms)
- Imagine how the child would react if he/she was not anxious

4.4.2.2 Sessions 3–7

These sessions addressed to child/adolescent are *educational* in essence: they are intended to teach her/him coping strategies (including relaxation, cognitive restructuring, combating avoidance) that s/he can use for the adequate self-management of anxiety. These sessions will include the following aspects:

The ABC of anxiety. The therapist will explore with the young patient how s/he believes the anxiety occurs. The therapist will make use of examples in which different persons react differently to the same situations, and emphasize that the evaluation of the situation truly makes the difference. The child/adolescent will be familiarized with the main irrational beliefs (namely, absolutistic demands, awfulizing/catastrophizing, low frustration tolerance, and global evaluation of self/others); therapist will use concrete examples to illustrate how these irrational beliefs stay at the core of the anxiety. Similarly, the therapist will teach the child/adolescents about rational beliefs (namely, preferences, non-awfulizing/non-catastrophizing, frustration tolerance, and contextual evaluation of behavior). The difference between rational and irrational beliefs will be evidenced on logical, empirical, and pragmatic bases, by means of using analogies, metaphors, stories, clinical vignettes, case examples. If the case, rational/irrational beliefs can be "personalized" as "good/bad birds trying to make nests in one's head," "butterflies" versus "gnats," etc. The patient will be encouraged to self-monitor her/his thoughts and try to identify thinking patterns related to emotional disturbance. The difference between functional and dysfunctional emotions will be reinforced, by pointing out that functional emotions are underlined by rational beliefs, while dysfunctional emotions are underlined by irrational ones. *Note*: If needed, therapist could choose to use alternative labels, as "useful/detrimental emotions" or "good/bad thoughts."

Controlling anxious arousal. Therapist will explain the young patient that the physiological arousal is under her/his control. If needed, therapist can explain how/why anxious arousal occurs and normalize the interpretations that child/adolescents assign to it. Most importantly, the therapist should demonstrate to the patient how the arousal can be induced and reduced by specific means (e.g., hyperventilation/respiration control). Progressive relaxation protocols and respiration control exercises can be used to teach the patient how to control anxious arousal. Importantly, the therapist should emphasize that acquiring the ability of easily control one's physiological activation requires extensive regular exercise—and plan with the patient the practice sessions of relaxation and respiration control exercises.

Controlling thoughts that generate anxiety: cognitive restructuring. Therapist will assist the child/adolescent in developing more realistically evaluations of the situations linked to anxiety, by means of: (1) challenging her/him to think about the specific consequences of the most feared scenario ("And if so, then what would happen?"); (2) challenging her/him to think about the consequences of the less feared scenario and/or the most desirable scenario; (3) helping her/him to balance the most and the less feared/most desirable scenario in such a way to identify the most probable one, realistically speaking. Similarly, therapist could ask the patient to think about how s/he would encourage a peer who would face a difficult situation and use this pretext to model adequate rational statements (e.g., if needed, the therapist will problematize the utility of statements like “Everything will be all right.” and will model alternative rational statements like “Do your best, it’s nothing more you can do”). Other possible strategies than can be used for cognitive restructuring include modeling and role playing.

How avoidance reinforces anxiety. The therapist will discuss with the patient about the motives behind our behaviors and illustrate the principle of positive/negative reinforcement using first neutral contents and/or case examples (see Sect. 4.5). Then, the therapist will discuss with the child/adolescent how avoidance negatively reinforce anxiety and worsen the situation for the patient, in that avoidance might make the feared negative consequences more probable (e.g., if the child/adolescent avoid a certain situation, s/he refuses herself/himself the chance of learning how to behave/perform in that situation, and thus the chances to really make mistakes increase). These principles can be illustrated by concrete examples/clinical vignettes.

Education and assistance for gradual exposure. The therapist will present exposure as the only efficient way of combating avoidance (in order to decrease anxiety) and teach the patients the principles of graded exposure (e.g., choosing a low-to-moderate challenging situation, and remain there despite discomfort, until the discomfort significantly diminishes). In-session imaginal exposure exercises will be undertaken; planning gradual exposure, direct or indirect modelling, and role playing of successful exposure can be also used.

Homework Suggestions for Sessions 3–7

- Practicing relaxation exercises
- Self-monitoring of irrational beliefs (in imagined or real-life anxiety-linked contexts)
- Imagine how a non-anxious peer would think in the very same situations in which the patient experiences anxiety
- Exposure to situations linked to low-to-moderate anxiety

4.4.2.3 First Parent Session

Parent sessions will be held separately from the sessions addressed to the child/adolescents. There are two parent sessions. First of them will be held during the initial phase of the treatment (weeks 3–7; the parent session can be programmed in the same week with one of the child/adolescent session, but only the parent will attend this meeting with the therapist) and will be designed to cover the following points:

Obtaining parent/legal guardian cooperation and support. Although parent/legal guardian usually expressed their consent for the psychotherapy prior to initiate it, this meeting with the parent is designed specifically to help parent realize s/he has a key role in supporting the therapeutic process, as s/he knows better his/her child and spend considerably more time with s/he.

Promoting parent's understanding of his/her child anxiety. The therapist will explain the parent how and why does anxiety occur and will counteract any eventual self-blame of the parent. Also, the therapist will assist parent to see the linkage of various anxiety symptoms of his/her child (e.g., marked distress, sleep disturbance, strange behaviors, etc.) as well as the linkage between anxiety and other eventual emotional problems.

Parental education for psychotherapy and REBT. The therapist will present the parent the REBT philosophy and explain how the psychotherapeutic process will unfold. In addition, the therapist will explain parent how s/he can assist their child/adolescent in overcoming anxiety, by means of adequate modelling, promoting rational beliefs, encouraging the child/adolescents prepare for and face difficult situations, promoting self-acceptance, facilitating the implementation of homework for therapeutic sessions, and rewarding the child/adolescents efforts in overcoming anxiety.

Adjusting treatment expectations. Two main aspects will be discussed here: (1) confidentiality issue: the therapist will make clear for the parent that s/he will not act for the parent as a source of information his/her child/adolescent do not want to share—except for cases of major force; and (2) treatment gains: the therapist will explain how treatment gains will be visible, when to expect them, as well as the fact that occasional problems/failures should be expected, and are normal.

The middle phase of the treatment (weeks 8–12) includes sessions 8–12, all addressed to the child/adolescent. These sessions are designed to provide the patient with the opportunity to systematically practice REBT principles to overcome anxiety in real life context. We detail below the structure recommended for every of these sessions:

Working on real-life anxiety-linked situation, based on the ABCDE model of REBT. The therapist will assist the patient to apply ABCDE model of REBT to real life situations. More specifically, after identifying the situations, the child/adolescent will identify his usual reactions (physiological, behavioral, and emotional) to that situations, as well as his rational/irrational cognitions. In case on irrational cognitions, s/he will use disputation to restructure them and replace them with rational ones. The child/adolescents will be encouraged to practice "offline" cognitive restructuring (e.g., when preparing for confronting an anxiety-linked situation), as well as "online" cognitive restructuring (e.g., by rehearsing rational beliefs while in real life anxiety-linked situations).

Working toward strengthening the child's rational beliefs and weakening the irrational beliefs. To this end, various therapeutic strategies could be used. For example, the child/adolescents will be encouraged to see patterns in his/her thinking and be aware of that irrational belief which disturbs her/him more often. Those irrational beliefs will be subject of extensive cognitive restructuring, using imaginary scenarios, past, or anticipated situations. The therapist may encourage the child/adolescents to make a "Restructuring Kit," by collecting aphorism, poetries, lyrics, photos, cognitive or behavioral exercises, and/or video materials which helped her/him to have certain "rational insights" and use it periodically to strengthen her/his rationality.

Teaching child strategies for overcoming common difficulties associated with implementing the treatment plan; problem solving skills. The therapist will teach the child/adolescent problem solving skills using neutral or anecdotic contents first. Then, the therapist will discuss with the patient common difficulties associated with implementing the treatment plan (e.g., not doing your homework, obtaining less than optimal results, etc.) and approach them from a problem solving perspective (i.e., What do I have now?/What is the problem?; What do I want?/What is my goal?; How can I get there?; Balancing possible solutions in terms of costs and benefits; Choosing an alternative and implement it; Evaluating the results, and reinitialize the process, if needed, or adjusting the goals).

Homework Suggestions for Sessions 8–12

- Using relaxation to control anxious arousal in real life situations
- Cognitive restructuring in real life situations, to control secondary emotions related to anxiety
- Cognitive restructuring in real life situations to control anxiety
- Planning and implementing exposure to real life anxiety-linked situations (moderate to high anxiety)
- Addressing possible obstacles and failures in reaching the desired goals: devising and implementing back-up plans in specific situations

The final phase of the treatment (weeks 13–14) includes the last two sessions addressed to the child/adolescent, as well as the second session addressed to parent(s). The last two sessions dedicated to the child/adolescent are aimed to two main aspect. First, the therapist will prepare the patient for the finalization of the therapeutic process, by encouraging him/her to take stock of the newly acquired knowledge and skills. In addition, the child/adolescent's successful attempts of managing his/her anxiety will be used to prove his/her autonomy and competence to control his/her own anxiety. Second, the therapist and patient will discuss the relapse possibility and devise plans for relapse prevention.

Homework Suggestions for the Last Two Sessions

- Summarizing what the patient learned during the therapy
- Devising plans for dealing with eventual relapses
- Rehearsing rational statement in real life situations

The final phase of the treatment includes also the second parent session, designed to provide the context for the therapist to discuss with the parent how the parent can support his/her child/adolescent in maintaining and generalizing the therapeutic gains, how to recognize a relapse, and how to support child/adolescent in case of relapse.

First Session Should Be Structured to Include

- Establishing a therapeutic relation with the child
- Setting the agenda (and providing a rationale for doing so)
- Doing a mood check (including objective scores)
- Briefly reviewing the presenting problems and obtaining an update (since evaluation)
- Establishing a list of problems and agreeing on therapeutic goals
- Educating the patient about psychotherapy
- Evaluating the child's knowledge about emotions (valence, intensity) and teaching him/her the distinction between functional/dysfunctional emotions
- Eliciting and adjusting child's expectations for psychotherapy
- Providing a summary
- Setting a homework
- Giving and eliciting feedback

Second Session Should Be Structured to Include

- Brief update and mood check
- Establishing the linkage with the previous session
- Reviewing homework
- Setting agenda
- Discuss anxiety as a dysfunctional emotion
- Discuss the linkage between anxiety and other possible secondary emotions
- Provide summary
- Assign homework
- Giving and eliciting feedback

Sessions Three and Beyond Should Be Structured to Include

- Brief update and mood check
- Establishing the linkage with the previous session
- Reviewing homework
- Setting agenda
- Working on particular problems on the agenda
- Provide summary
- Assign homework
- Giving and eliciting feedback

First Parent Session Should Be Structured to Include

- Setting the agenda (and providing a rationale for doing so)
- Obtaining parent's view of the child's present problems
- Educating the parent about anxiety and the REBT model
- Educating the parent about psychotherapy and how (s)he should support the psychotherapeutic process (with an emphasis on modelling rational cognitions and adaptive behavior, as well as providing a structured environment and rewards the child's efforts to overcome anxiety)

- Establishing a cooperative relationship with the parent
- Eliciting and adjusting parent's expectations for psychotherapy
- Providing a summary
- Giving and eliciting feedback

Second Parent Session Should Be Structured to Include

- Setting the agenda (and providing a rationale for doing so)
- Obtaining parent's view of the therapeutic process and answering any parent's questions
- Discussing how parents will support their child in maintaining the therapeutic gains, and what they can do in case of relapse
- Providing a summary
- Giving and eliciting feedback

4.5 Therapist Resources

4.5.1 Explaining the Difference Between Functional and Dysfunctional Emotions (with an Emphasis on Anxiety and Fear)

In everyday life, all of us experience emotions. Some of them feel good (i.e., are positive emotions), other feel bad (e.g., are negative emotions). Emotions are like security systems, which tell us if everything goes as expected. Most of us would like to have exclusively positive emotions—because they feel good. However, negative emotions are necessary as well. Let me explain you: negative emotions feel bad, right? Pain also feel bad. But what would happen if your body does not have the ability to feel pain? Most probably, your body would be destroyed soon by negative factors in the environment—imagine what would happen if you don't notice the pain provoked by a burn or by a serious injury! But when you feel the pain, you know something is wrong and take action to reverse the negative consequences of what's going wrong. It's the same for emotions: negative emotions are good (or useful) because they let you know you should make some changes in order to regain the well-being and be able to reach your goals. Moreover, despite the widespread belief that positive emotions are always useful and desirable, it is not necessarily so: in fact, striving for obtaining positive emotions no matter what might be detrimental. Imagine a person who uses drugs or alcohol in order to obtain temporary emotional relief: on the long shot, this will diminish her/his capacity to live a productive and happy life.

Therefore, emotions are not good or bad because they are positive or negative! Both positive and negative emotions can be useful (good) or useless/detrimental (bad), depending on their function: do they help you to be in control of your life or do they hamper your ability to looking forward to reach your goals? We already pointed out how negative emotions can be useful and how positive emotions can be detrimental. But what about detrimental negative emotions? Or when do negative emotions become detrimental? It's simple: when they last unreasonably long, affect your performance, and impede you to enjoy experiences or to reach your goals. To figure out if an emotion (positive or negative) helps you or not, you can make use of the guidelines below:

Useful emotions	Detrimental emotions
• Helps you to realistically note what's going wrong (or good) in your life	• Impede you to realistically assess the reality (you have a distorted perception of what's going in your life)
• Serve you to resolve the negative situation (or adequately enjoy the positive one)	• Interfere with your capacity of reaching your goals
	• Make you avoid or inadequately ignore the problem

Fear	Anxiety
• You assess realistically the threat	• You overestimate the threat
• You assess realistically your capacity of facing the threat	• You underestimate your capacity of facing it
• You don't create a bigger threat in your mind (don't exaggerate the magnitude of the threat)	• You amply the threat in your mind (e.g., you create terrible scenarios)
• You don't remember many irrelevant thoughts and situations	• You remember a lot of irrelevant thoughts and situations, which contribute to amplify the threat
• You approach the problem and resolve it	• You tend to avoid the feared situation
	• You rely excessively on others to face the feared situation

4.5.2 *Being in Control of Your Body: Controlling Anxious Arousal*

One of the modalities to get in control of our bodily reactions is to control your breath. You almost sure heard someone telling you when you were angry or nervous to take a deep breath! Similarly, you observed for sure that we breathe differently in different situations—think about how one breathes when tired or exercising compared with watching television, reading, or sleeping. Or just think about how someone breathes when scared. The thing is the more relaxed you are, the more regular you breathe. And it is not regularity only—it's how you exhale, and how often you repeat the cycle of inspire and exhale that help you to relax. Why? Because a slower rate of breathing and a more profound exhalation lowers the oxygen sent to your muscles, causing them to relax. If you don't believe me, remember how you react when you play hide and seeking, and the person who's looking for you passes nearer your hiding place: you tend to retain your breath for the moment; after s/he's away, you slowly exhale all the air and experience a relief. That's relaxation. And you can cultivate it simply by controlling your breathing. The idea is to inhale normally, but let the air out slowly, prolonging the process as much as possible. After 20–25 such cycles of breathing, you can start to decrease the rate of the breathing, by inserting a short pause between inhaling and exhaling—that's means to retain your breath for 4–5 s. As you doing this, you can repeat a word in your mind—like "calm," "peace," or "easy." By doing this, you'll associate the relaxation state with calm breathing in such a way that next time when you want to relax, your body will start already to relax when you say yourself the "magical" word.

4.5.3 Spin Thoughts Key: How Your Thoughts Make You Anxious

We cannot control everything; sometimes bad things happen and we can do nothing about it—sometimes, for example, parents or friends can be angry with us and we don't know why. Other times, we fear something bad will happen and we don't know what to do or don't know if we can solve the problem, like when we are about to take a test and we fear we will fail. Sometimes our fear is so big that we cannot concentrate and do the right thing. In these cases, remember that our thoughts control what we feel and remember the ABC model.

A = **A**ctivating event or situation that we experience (e.g., taking a test)

↓

B = **B**eliefs or thoughts regarding the situation (e.g., I will get a bad grade, my parents will be mad, and my colleagues will laugh at me)

↓

C = **C**onsequence: How we feel or act based on these beliefs (e.g., anxious, panicked, not being able to focus)

So, every time you feel anxious or distressed, pay attention to your thoughts, to what you are telling yourself. When you notice unhelpful thoughts, you should ask yourself:

- Does believing like this (e.g., that I will fail and it will be awful) help you?
- Is this belief true? Be a detective and try to find out if your belief is true, by gathering evidence pro and against it (e.g., if you got a bad grade before, was that so awful, like the end of the world?)

- Does this belief make sense? How come a bad event becomes the worst case scenario? If a friend held such thoughts and asked you for advice, what would you tell him?

4.5.4 Gain Control over Your Behavior: Overcome Avoidance

When we fear something, we usually try to avoid it, and this is normally a reasonable thing to do. Like when we are standing near the edge of a cliff and we look down, fear makes us step back so we don't fall. Falling down a cliff is a real danger, so we'd better avoid it. But sometimes, the dangers are just in our heads (e.g., when you believe that your colleagues do not like you even if you don't really know) or they exist, but they are not life-threatening, unlikely, or not even that bad (e.g., playing with a dog might end with us being bit but that is very unlikely when we play with dogs we know). Avoiding them only leads to increased fear because this way we cannot learn that we can deal with it and move on. What would happen if we avoided taking tests? Would that make us better students? What would happen if you were afraid to ride a bike, thinking you will make mistakes and fall, and you would avoid all attempts? Would you ever learn? So, remember not to avoid feared situations just because you fear them; ask yourself (and when unsure, ask your parents or teachers) if the danger is real, and if it is not (or if it is, but it's not worth avoiding, like taking a test), confront it.

You can confront it easier if you (1) take small steps, (2) practice every step until you are not afraid or much less so—use your breathing exercises. You can use a similar chart like the one below, which is an example for a child who was very much afraid of dogs at first but managed to control his fear.

	How much you fear it at first	How much you fear it afterwards
	1—not at all	1—not at all
Steps you want to take	10—very much	10—very much
Looking at the photo of a dog	2	1
Watch the movie Lassie	3	1
Looking at a dog from a distance, with your parents	4	2
Go to the pet store and look at a puppy	5	2
Go to the pet store and hold/play with the puppy for 5 min	5	2
Visit a friend who has a dog and watch it/play with it while it is leashed	7	3
Play with your friend's dog for 5 min	7	2

4.5.5 Remain in the Control of Your Emotions!

To remain in the control of your emotions, you need to "remain in good shape." That means you need to exercise regularly strategies that allow you to adequately react to difficult (un)expected situations. You can use the graphic below to plan what you'll do to remain in good psychological shape:

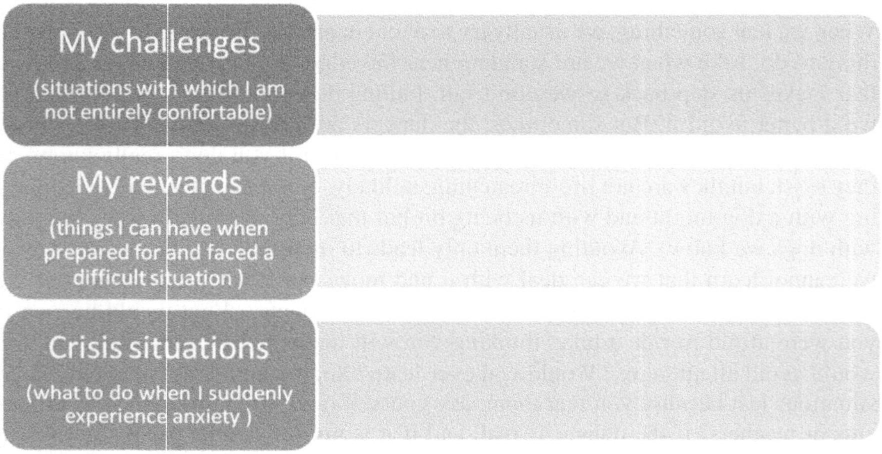

Acknowledgments This chapter was funded by the Romanian Executive Unit for Financing Education Higher Research, Development and Innovation (UEFISCDI) via the "Effectiveness of an empirically based web platform for anxiety in youths" grant, number PN-II-PT-PCCA-2011-3.1-1500, 81/2012 coordinated by Dr. Anca Dobrean.

References

Bandura, A. (Ed.). (1977). *Social learning theory*. Englewood Cliffs, NJ: Prentice-Hall.

Barlow, D. H. (2002). *Anxiety and its disorders: The nature and treatment of anxiety and panic* (2nd ed.). New York: Guilford.

Beck, A. T. (1976). *Cognitive therapy and the emotional disorders*. New York: International Universities Press.

Bernard, M. E., & Joyce, M. R. (1984). *Rational emotive therapy with children and adolescents*. New York: Wiley.

Cartwright-Hatton, S., Roberts, C., Chitsabesan, P., Fothergill, C., & Harrington, R. (2004). Systematic review of the efficacy of cognitive behaviour therapies for childhood and adolescent anxiety disorders. *British Journal of Clinical Psychology, 43*, 421–436.

Clark, D. A., & Beck, A. T. (2010). *Cognitive therapy of anxiety disorders. Science and practice*. New York: Guilford.

Creswell, C., Murray, L., Stacey, J., & Cooper, P. (2011). Parenting and child anxiety. In W. K. Silverman & A. P. Field (Eds.), *Anxiety disorders in children and adolescents* (2nd ed.). Cambridge, England: Cambridge Child and Adolescent Psychiatry, Cambridge University Press.

DiGiuseppe, R., & Bernard, M. (2006). REBT assessment and treatment with children. In A. Ellis & M. Bernard (Eds.), *Rational emotive behavioral approaches to childhood disorders. Theory, practice, and research* (pp. 85–114). New York: Springer.

Ellis, A. (1994). *Reason and emotion in psychotherapy* (Rev. ed.). Secaucus, NJ: Birch Lane.

Ellis, A. (1982). Psychoneurosis and anxiety problems. In R. Grieger and I. Grieger's (eds.), *Cognition and emotional disturbance*. New York: Human Sciences Press.

Ellis, A. & Bernard, M. (2006). *Rational emotive behavioral approaches to childhood disorders (Theory, practice, and research)*. New York: Springer.

Iftene, F., Predescu, E., Stefan, S., & David, D. (2015). Rational-emotive and cognitive-behavior therapy (REBT/CBT) versus pharmacotherapy versus REBT/CBT plus pharmacotherapy in the treatment of major depressive disorder in youth; A randomized clinical trial. *Psychiatry Research, 225*(3), 687–692.

James, A. C., James, G., Cowdrey, F. A., Soler, A., & Choke, A. (2013). Cognitive behavioural therapy for anxiety disorders in children and adolescents. *Cochrane Database of Systematic Reviews,* (6), CD004690.

James, A., Soler, A., & Weatherall, R. (2005). Cognitive behavioural therapy for anxiety disorders in children and adolescents. *Cochrane Database of Systematic Reviews,* (4), CD004690.

Kendall, P. C. (1994). Treating anxiety disorders in children: Results of a randomized clinical trial. *Journal of Consulting and Clinical Psychology, 62*(1), 100–110.

Kendall, P. C., & Southam-Gerow, M. A. (1996). Long-term follow-up of a cognitive-behavioral therapy for anxiety-disordered youth. *Journal of Consulting and Clinical Psychology, 64*(4), 724–730.

March, J., Parker, J., Sullivan, K., Stallings, P., & Conners, C. (1997). The Multidimensional Anxiety Scale for Children (MASC): Factor structure, reliability and validity. *Journal of the American Academy of Child and Adolescent Psychiatry, 36*, 554–565.

Marshall, T., & Ramchandani, T. (2008). Emotional disorders in children and adolescents. *Medicine, 36*(9), 478–481.

Shortt, A. L., Barrett, P. M., & Fox, T. L. (2001). Evaluating the FRIENDS program: A cognitive-behavioral group treatment for anxious children and their parents. *Journal of Child Clinical Psychology, 30*(4), 525–535.

Silverman, W. K., & Motoca, L. M. (2011). Treatment: An update and recommendations. In W. K. Silverman & A. P. Field (Eds.), *Anxiety disorders in children and adolescents* (2nd ed.). New York: Cambridge University Press.

Silverman, W. K., Pina, A. A., & Viswesvaran, C. (2008). Evidence-based psychosocial treatments for phobic and anxiety disorders in children and adolescents. *Journal of Clinical Child and Adolescent Psychology, 37*, 105–130.

Skinner, B. F. (1974). *About behaviorism*. New York: Random House.

Spence, S. H. (1998). A measure of anxiety symptoms among children. *Behavior Research and Therapy, 36*, 545–566.

Wagner, K. D., Ambrosini, P., Rynn, M., Wohlberg, C., Yang, R., Greenbaum, M. S., et al. (2003). Efficacy of sertraline in the treatment of children and adolescents with major depressive disorder. Two randomized controlled trials. *The Journal of the American Medical Association, 290*(8), 103–1041.

Watson, J. B., & Rayner, R. (1920). Conditioned emotional reactions. *Journal of Experimental Psychology, 3*, 1–14.

Woulff, N. (1983). Involving the family in the treatment of the child: A model for rational-emotive therapists. In A. Ellis & M. E. Bernard (Eds.), *Rational-emotive approaches to the problems of childhood*. New York: Plenum Press.

Chapter 5
Rational Stories for Children. A Rational Emotive Education Protocol for Approaching Anxiety in Children and Adolescents Based on the Stories Book *The Retmagic and Wonderful Adventures of Retman*

Cognitive-Behavioral Therapies (CBT) are currently considered (Hofmann, Asnaani, Vonk, Sawyer, & Fang, 2012) effective treatments for child and adolescent psychopathology. The very first form of CBT is Rational-Emotive and Cognitive-Behavior Therapy (RE&CBT Ellis, 1962).

5.1 The Cognitive-Behavioral Conceptualization of Child and Adolescent Anxiety

RE&CBT conceptualizes child internalizing or externalizing psychopathology (DiGiuseppe & David, 2015; Ellis, Wolfe, & Moseley, 1966) as dysfunctional responses based on irrational thinking and maladaptive patterns learned from their environment, which are then working as endogenous vulnerability factors.

Irrational cognitions represent the central focus of the RE&CBT, being categorized (DiGiuseppe & David, 2015) into: demandingness (DEM; e.g., when a child thinks "I must be approved"), awfulizing/catastrophyzing (AWF; e.g., "Since I was rejected, it is awful."), self-downing (SD; e.g., "I am unliked and thus worthless"), and low frustration tolerance (LFT; "I can't stand this situation"). Irrational thinking has been documented in the literature (see Ellis, David, & Lynn, 2010) to be associated with dysfunctional emotions and maladaptive behavioral reactions. Hence, there are rational alternative thinking patterns tought by REBT/CBT for promoting healthy emotions in children and adolescents, in the form of preferences (PREF) rather than DEM, badness (BAD) rather than AWF, unconditional self-acceptance (USA) rather than SD, and frustration tolerance (FT) rather than LFT.

I.A. Cristea et al., *REBT in the Treatment of Anxiety Disorders in Children and Adults*, SpringerBriefs in Psychology, DOI 10.1007/978-3-319-18419-7_5

5.2 CBT and RE&CBT for Approaching Child and Adolescent Anxiety: Formats

Considering the ethipathogenetic factors mentioned above, RE&CBT has focused on addressing maladaptive emotion-regulation strategies in both children and their parents (Gavita, David, Bujoreanu, Tiba, & Ionutiu, 2012; Gavita, David, & DiGiuseppe, 2014; Gavita, DiGiuseppe, & David, 2013). Although cognitive-behavioral interventions have been extensively documented in recent years, there is yet little research to comparatively investigate which are the most effective modalities for delivering them (e.g., directly to children, using parents as agents of change, and/or both) when addressing child psychopathology.

Various types of child interventions (e.g., individual or group), interventions including parents and/or teacher as agents of change, have been implemented with positive results. Group formats of CBT/RE&CBT are currently considered (NICE, 2006) effective means of addressing child and adolescent psychopathology. Compared to individual therapy, group interventions offer children increased opportunities for vicarious learning and peer-support for modifying cognitions, emotions, and maladaptive behaviors.

Rational Emotive & Cognitive-Behavioral Education (previously called Rational Emotive Education; REE) was from RE&CBT in 1970s as a prevention curricula for working with children (Kanus, 2004). REE can be delivered in classroom formats (or other teacher-delivered formats) and various experiential lessons were developed (Vernon, 2004) for teaching children emotion-regulation skills. REE has proved to be effective (Trip, Vernon, & McMahon, 2007) in both prevention of psychopathology in children and adolescents, but also for approaching internalizing (e.g., anxiety disorders; $d=.80$) or externalizing problems.

5.3 Therapeutic Stories and Rational Stories

Stories can be considered traditional methods for modeling behaviors by means of metaphors. They were used long before current evidence-based treatments for child psychopathology existed, and thus therapy found a source of inspiration in its metaphors. Therefore, RE&CBT incorporated since its beginnings (Waters, 1980) therapeutic stories in the treatment of child psychopathology and called them rational stories. Thus, rational stories are based on metaphoric content and are considered (see Parker & Wampler, 2006; Pomerantz, 2006) effective means for approaching child psychopathology.

Rational stories are aiming to teach children rational thinking patterns in order to cope effectively with negative events and exhibit adaptive emotional and behavioral reactions. The REBT/CBT therapeutic stories are offering a modeling role through their characters for child behaviors. Moreover, it was proposed that they are helping children to reflect and take an active stance for changing their own thinking, emotions and behaviors, solving problems, reducing resistance, and enhancing motivation. Currently, therapeutic stories are used independently or within other programs delivered to children or their parents (e.g., homework, bibliotherapy).

5.4 Clinical Assessment Tools

- Achenbach System of Empirically Based Assessment (ASEBA; Achenbach & Rescorla, 2000, 2001), Child Behavior Checklist (CBCL), and Teacher Report Form (TRF) 6–18, for measuring internalizing and externalizing syndromes and DSM-oriented scales (e.g., anxiety problems).
- Spence Children's Anxiety Scale (Spence et al., 2000), for measuring parent- or teacher-reported child anxiety.
- Functional and Dysfunctional Child Mood Scales (FD-CMS; Gavita & Neamtu, in preparation; see Appendix) for measuring child-reported anxiety, worry, distress, and positive emotions. FD-CMD is a 9-item scale with a version for girls and one for boys using images to suggest the display of each emotion. The scale is based on the binary model of emotional distress (David, Montgomery, Macavei, & Bovbjerg, 2005) and assesses the intensity of children's and adolescent's emotional experiences on a 10-point scale, with images that correspond to the emotions that they had.
- Emotion Regulation Index for Children and Adolescents (ERICA; MacDermott, Gullone, Allen, King & Tonge, 2010), for measuring emotional control, emotional awareness, and emotional receptivity.
- The Child and Adolescent Scale of Irrationality 1 (CASI; Bernard & Cronan, 1999) for measuring irrational cognitions in children and adolescents.

5.5 The RETMAN's Rational Stories Protocol for Child and Adolescent Anxiety

The RETMAN's rational stories protocol consists of nine sessions of group sessions with children and adolescents using the stories and comics from the book "*The Retmagic and wonderful adventures of Retman*" (David, 2010).

The purpose of this group-based RE&CBT is to educate group members concerning on their thoughts that influence the emotions and behaviors and identify and change irrational thinking by using disputing strategies. According to the "ABC(DE)" model of RE&CBT (Ellis, 1962, 1994), children perceive undesirable activating event (A) about which children have rational or irrational beliefs (B). Rational beliefs lead to functional consequences and irrational beliefs lead to dysfunctional consequences (C). In the next step, children are learning to dispute (D) their dysfunctional beliefs and to assimilate (E) new functional and rational beliefs. The REBT techniques used to help children and the adolescents to practice these skills include storytelling, modeling, role play, imagery, themes which involve the adults, offering some books as bibliotherapy and for the written homework, practicing the slogans for rational coping in the form of "psychological pills" (David, 2006; Gavita et al., 2013).

This intervention was tested by Gavita and Calin (2013) in a sample of primary school children over 3 weeks, with three 40-min sessions each week (a total of nine sessions during the 3 weeks). Results showed that the REE intervention based on the RETMAN protocol reduced internalizing and externalizing syndromes in children. Moreover, children reported a lower level of irrational thinking after participating in the intervention.

5.5.1 Key Elements of the Protocol

The REBT intervention was developed based on the rational stories for children and adolescents "*Retmagic and the wonderful adventures of RETMAN*" (David, 2010). The REE protocol integrated (Gavita & Calin, 2013) stories from the book as stimulus activities for raising awareness on the connection and causal links between irrational beliefs (IBs) and emotional problems, and practicing rational beliefs (RBs).

RETMAN is a cartoon character developed for making the principles of RE&CBT more accessible among children and adolescents. The first RETMAN concept was developed at the Albert Ellis Institute, USA, in the 1980s (Merriefield & Merriefield, 1979), and was inspired by the name Rational Emotive Therapy (RET was the name used at the time for current REBT).

RETMAN was "reloaded" by David in 2010, with the character having his own story (e.g., he is coming from a planet called Rationalia) and adventures in the book called "Retmagic and the wonderful adventures of RETMAN" (see for details http://www.retman.ro). For the original RETMAN story, see here http://www.psychotherapy.ro/meet-retman/the-retmagic-of-retman/.

5.5.2 The Content of the RETMAN's Rational Stories

In the book, RETMAN takes the stance of a wizard psychotherapist, who helps children when they are suffering (i.e., anxiety) and teaches them how to be happy (by practicing rational beliefs). The "magic" that RETMAN practice is called "Retmagic," and it is embedded in its five "secrets" for a healthy mood. To help children to be healthy and happy, RETMAN fights with the Wizard Irationalius, and his helpers: Necessarus, Descurajatus, Catastrofus, Frustratus, characters that correspond with irrational beliefs of children. With the help of RETMAN, children discover the five secrets of happiness, including the Great Secret ABC-relationship between situation, thought, and emotion. RETMAN summarizes its "secrets" after the stories in the form of PsyPills ("psychological pills") for children (David, 2006; see Appendix).

5.5.3 *Session Structure*

The intervention is delivered in a group setting of 6–12 children/adolescents, based on the RETMAN rational stories (David, 2010). Each session is based on reading a story from the book and discussing the actions of the great wizard therapist, following the format of the Rational Emotive Education experiential lessons (Vernon, 2004).

Session format (session 1–9):

- Brief update and mood check
- Bridge from previous session
- Review homework
- Session objectives
- Stimulus story
- Discussions (content and personalizing questions)
- Session summary
- Homework assignment
- Feedback

The rational stories are following the typical stages of a therapeutic story (see Painter, Cook, & Silverman, 1999):

- Introducing the main character.
- Identifying the problem.
- Discussion with the wise character (in this case RETMAN).
- Testing the alternatives and summarizing tale's learning conclusion.

The main themes included in the RETMAN intervention sessions were:

- Understanding the connection between thinking and feeling.
- How irrational thoughts are causing unhealthy emotions.
- How to change irrational thinking with rational thinking.
- The consequences of rational thinking.
- How RETMAN teaches children to think rationally.
- Homework—stories and PsyPills.

At the end of each session, each child receives a PsyPill (David, 2006) for practicing newly acquired rational thinking strategies when feeling distressed. The roboRETMAN robot can be used within sessions for giving the PsyPill to the child and the PsyPills app is suitable for being used by adolescents between sessions for practicing their rational thinking strategies. At the end of each session children received as homework (1) the story, the comics RETMAN (see here http://www.psychotherapy.ro/meet1retman/the1retmagic1of1retman/), and the PsyPills—how to get rid of anxiety, depression and anger—to read with their parents, (2) a form containing a game based on the main characters in the story to be solved at home, (3) the ABC(DE) form for registering the thoughts during the problematic situations, or (4) drawing an advertising poster to differentiate our world from the RETMAN world.

The last group session consists of a play organized based on the first story in the book, namely "A visit on the Rationalia," in which the children play the main characters.

Appendix

PsyPills for the Retman group (Gavita & Calin, 2013; based on David, 2010)
"Psychological pill" for regulating anxiety, panic, fear, and worry:

I would like things to be different, but I know that my wish does not necessarily come true just because I want to.
I can accept the fact that in life bad or unwanted things can happen to me, even if it is unpleasant and I did everything possible to avoid them.
It is very unpleasant that something like this happened to me, but it is not the worst thing possible.
I think I can handle even worse situations than what I am facing now.
It is very unpleasant, but is not awful if in this situation I will not be able to be in control like I would want to.
It is bad but not catastrophic to feel this kind of emotions.
It is unpleasant but not awful to have this type of thoughts.

Functional and Dysfunctional Child Mood Scales (girls version; developed by Gavita)

Instruction: Please circle the number between 0 and 10 which best corresponds to the way in which you have felt on the previous couple of weeks (this week/today/now) 0 means that you not felt at all that way and 10 means that you velt very much that way.

Sad

0 1 2 3 4 5 6 7 8 9 10

Depressed

0 1 2 3 4 5 6 7 8 9 10

Worried

0 1 2 3 4 5 6 7 8 9 10

Scared

0 1 2 3 4 5 6 7 8 9 10

Annoyed

0 1 2 3 4 5 6 7 8 9 10

Angry

0 1 2 3 4 5 6 7 8 9 10

Confident

0 1 2 3 4 5 6 7 8 9 10

Happy

0 1 2 3 4 5 6 7 8 9 10

Calm and relaxed

0 1 2 3 4 5 6 7 8 9 10

Functional and Dysfunctional Child Mood Scales
(developed by Gavita; boys version)

Instruction: Please circle the number between 0 and 10 which best corresponds to the way in which you have felt on the previous couple of weeks (this week/today/now) 0 means that you not felt at all that way and 10 means that you velt very much that way.

Sad

0 1 2 3 4 5 6 7 8 9 10

Depressed

0 1 2 3 4 5 6 7 8 9 10

Worried

0 1 2 3 4 5 6 7 8 9 10

Scared

0 1 2 3 4 5 6 7 8 9 10

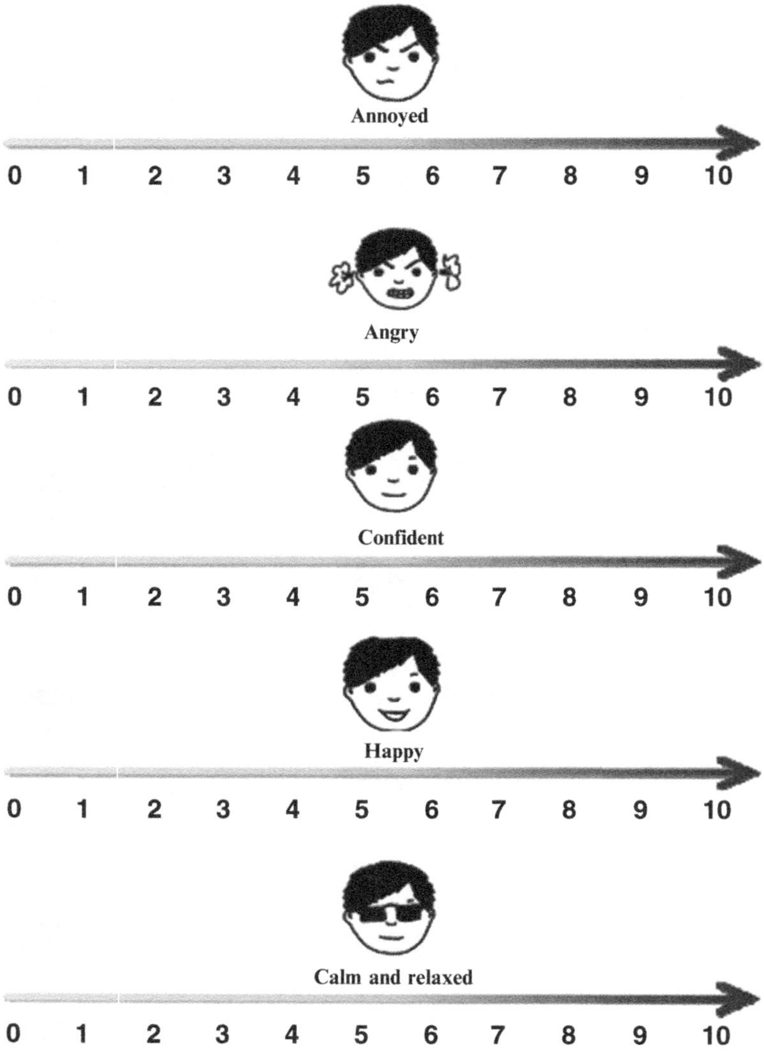

References

Achenbach, T. M., & Rescorla, L. A. (2000). *Manual for the ASEBA Preschool Forms & Profiles*. Burlington, VT: University of Vermont, Research Center for Children, Youth, & Families.

Achenbach, T. M., & Rescorla, L. A. (2001). *Manual for the ASEBA school-age forms & profiles*. Burlington, VT: Research Center for Children, Youth, & Families, University of Vermont.

Bernard, M. E., & Cronan, F. (1999). The Child and Adolescent Scale of Irrationality: Validation data and mental health correlates. *Journal of Cognitive Psychotherapy: An International Quarterly, 13*, 121–132.

David, D. (2006). *Handbook of cognitive and behavioral psychotherapies [Tratat de psihoterapii cognitive şi comportamentale]*. Iasi, Romania: Polirom.

David, D. (2010). *Retmagic and the wonderful adventures of RETMAN*. Cluj Napoca, Romania: RTS.

David, D., Montgomery, G. H., Macavei, B., & Bovbjerg, D. (2005). An empirical investigation of Albert Ellis' binary model of distress. *Journal of Clinical Psychology, 61*, 499–516.

DiGiuseppe, R., & David, O. A. (2015). Rational emotive behavior therapy. In T. Prout & D. T. Brown (Eds.), *Counseling and psychotherapy with children and adolescents: Theory and practice for school and clinical settings* (5th ed., pp. 155–214). New York: Wiley.

Ellis, A. (1962). *Reason and emotion in psychotherapy*. New York: Lyle Stuart.

Ellis, A. (1994). *Reason and emotion in psychotherapy* (Rev. ed.). Secaucus, NJ: Birch Lane

Ellis, A., David, D., & Lynn, J. S. (2010). Rational and irrational beliefs: A historical and conceptual perspective. In D. David, S. J. Lynn, & A. Ellis (Eds.), *Rational and irrational beliefs: Research, theory and clinical practice* (pp. 3–23). New York: Oxford University Press.

Ellis, A., Wolfe, J., & Moseley, S. (1966). *How to raise an emotionally healthy, happy child*. New York: Crown.

Gavita, O. A., & Calin, A. (2013). RETMAN rational stories versus rational parenting program for the treatment of child psychopathology: Efficacy of two formats of rational-emotive behavior therapy. *Journal of Cognitive and Behavioral Psychotherapies, 13*(1), 33–56.

Gavita, O. A., David, D., Bujoreanu, S., Tiba, A., & Ionutiu, D. R. (2012). The efficacy of a short cognitive-behavioral parent program in the treatment of externalizing behavior disorders in Romanian foster care children: Building parental emotion-regulation through unconditional self- and child-acceptance strategies. *Children and Youth Services Review, 34*(2), 1290–1297.

Gavita, O. A., David, D., & DiGiuseppe, R. (2014). You are such a bad child! Appraisals as mechanisms of parental negative and positive affect. *Journal of General Psychology, 141*(2), 113–129.

Gavita, O. A., DiGiuseppe, R., & David, D. (2013). Self-acceptance and raising children: The case of parental unconditional acceptance. In M. E. Bernard (Ed.), *The strength of self-acceptance*. New York: Springer.

Hofmann, S. G., Asnaani, A., Vonk, I. J. J., Sawyer, A. T., & Fang, A. (2012). The efficacy of cognitive behavioral therapy: A review of meta-analyses. *Cognitive Therapy and Research, 36*(5), 427–440. doi:10.1007/s10608-012-9476-1.

Kanus, W. (2004). Rational emotive education: Trends and directions. *Romanian Journal of Cognitive and Behavioral Psychotherapies, 4*(1), 9–22.

MacDermott, S. T., Gullone, E., Allen, J. S., King, N. J., & Tonge, B. (2010). The Emotion Regulation Index for Children and Adolescents (ERICA): A psychometric investigation. Journal of Psychopathology and Behavioral Assessment, 32, 301–314.

Merriefield, C., & Merriefield, R. (1979). *Call me Ret-man and have a ball*. New York: Institute for Rational Living.

NICE (National Institute for Health and Clinical Excellence). (2006). *NICE technology appraisal guidance, parent-training/education programmes in the management of children with conduct disorders*. London: NICE.

Painter, L.T., Cook, J. W., & Silverman, P.S. (1999). The effects of therapeutic storytelling and behavioral parent training on noncompliant behavior in young boys. *Child and Family Behavior Therapy, 21*, 2, 47–66.

Parker, T. S., & Wampler, K. S. (2006). Changing emotion: The use of therapeutic storytelling. *Journal of Marital and Family Therapy, 32*(2), 155–166.

Pomerantz, K. A. (2006). Helping children explore their emotional and social worlds through therapeutic stories. *Educational and Child Psychology, 24*(1), 46–55.

Spence, S., Donovan, C., & Brechman-Toussaint, M. (2000). The treatment of childhood social phobia: The effectiveness of a social skills training-based, cognitive behavioural intervention, with and without parental involvement. *Journal of Child Psychology and Psychiatry and Allied Disciplines, 41*(6), 713–726.

Trip, S., Vernon, A., & McMahon, J. (2007). Effectiveness of rational emotive education: A quantitative meta-analytical study. *Journal of Cognitive and Behavioral Psychotherapies, 7*, 81–93.

Vernon, A. (2004). Rational-emotive education. *Romanian Journal of Cognitive and Behavioral Psychotherapies, 4*(1), 23–37.

Waters, V. (1980). *Rational stories for children*. New York: Albert Ellis Institute.

The manufacturer's authorised representative in the EU is Springer Nature Customer Service Centre GmbH, Europaplatz 3, 69115 Heidelberg, Germany. If you have any concerns regarding our products, please contact ProductSafety@springernature.com

Printed and bound by CPI Group (UK) Ltd, Croydon, CR0 4YY
30/09/2026
02225606-0008